Literary Ideas and Scripts for Young Playwrights

Lisa Kaniut Cobb

Illustrated by Helen Matthews

TEACHER IDEAS PRESS
Portsmouth, NH

To all my friends who teach
and their students who write.

Teacher Ideas Press
A division of Reed Elsevier Inc.
361 Hanover Street
Portsmouth, NH 03801–3912
www.teacherideaspress.com

Offices and agents throughout the world

© 2004 by Lisa Kanuit Cobb

All rights reserved. No part of this book may be reproduced in any form or by any electronic or mechanical means, including information storage and retrieval systems, without permission in writing from the publisher, except by a reviewer, who may quote brief passages in a review.

The author and publisher wish to thank those who have generously given permission to reprint borrowed material:

"in Just-" from *Complete Poems: 1904–1962* by E. E. Cummings, edited by George J. Firmage. Copyright © 1923, 1951, 1991 by the Trustees for the E. E. Cummings Trust. Copyright © 1976 by George James Firmage. Used by permission of Liveright Publishing Corporation.

Library of Congress Cataloging-in-Publication Data

Cobb, Lisa Kaniut.
   Literary ideas and scripts for young playwrights / Lisa Kaniut Cobb.
     p. cm.
   Includes bibliographical references and index.
    ISBN 1-59158-071-4
    1. Children's theater—Juvenile literature. 2. Playwriting—Juvenile literature. 3. Children's plays, American. I. Title.
PN3157.C58 2004
792'.0226—dc22   2003020550

Editor: Suzanne Barchers
Production: Angela Laughlin
Typesetter: Westchester Book Services
Cover design: Susan Geer
Manufacturing: Steve Bernier

Printed in the United States of America on acid-free paper

08 07 06 05 04   VP   1 2 3 4 5

Contents

List of Forms v

Acknowledgments vii

Introduction ix

1. Poetry for Choral Readings 1
    Mudluscious 4
    The Sunny Night 13

2. Fairy Tales for Readers Theatre 19
    The Last Toll 21

3. Fairy Tale Plays 29
    Jack and the Beanstalk 31
    Hansel and Gretel 39

4. Fairy Tale Variations for Readers Theatre 51
    The Three Snapping Turtles 53

5. Fairy Tale Variations for Plays 59
    Sally's Seven Chefs 61

6. Modern Fairy Tale Plays 73
    The Secret of Success 77

7. Story Joke Plays 87
    Some Luck 90

8. Poetry Plays 99
    All the Difference 101
    Once Upon a Midnight Dreary 112

9. Historical Plays 119
    The Midnight Ride of Paul Revere 122

10.	Cultural Myth Plays	137
	Fire and Water	140
11.	Original Story Plays	157
	Agent Eleven: Guard Dog Extraordinaire	161

Glossary 175

Index 177

About the Author and the Illustrator 179

List of Forms

Form 3.1	Script Planning Sheet	48
Form 6.1	Script Adaptation Sheet	85
Form 8.1	Questionnaire for Clustering a Poem to a Play	117
Form 11.1	Critique Guidelines	170
Form 11.2	Play Evaluation Rubric	173

Acknowledgments

Many people were instrumental in the evolution of this book. Thank you Lola Todd, Lynn Ackerman, Susan Roup, and Jenny Slater for inviting me into your classrooms to lead writing projects, and especially for your wonderful, imaginative, and cooperative students. Thank you students at Summit View Elementary School for inspiring many of the stories that have been adapted here into plays. Thank you, Karen Moore, for believing enough in this writing program to find room in your budget; Karen Forbes for space and time in your library; and Mark Phillips for technical assistance.

My professors at the University of Denver's University College inspired and encouraged my writing through their classes, especially my capstone advisor, Andy Rooney. Thank you as well to my friends in the Rocky Mountain Chapter of the Society of Children's Book Writers and Illustrators and to Jackie Turner, Traci Jones, and Helen Matthews for gently steering my work over the years. Helen Matthews is also responsible for the wonderful illustrations throughout the book. Thank you, Suzanne Barchers, for encouraging me to write plays and permitting me to include creative writing ideas.

Of course, my most immediate support came from Wesley, Ashley, Charles, and Libby. They never complained about late suppers or dusty tables as I barricaded myself in my office, clicking away at the keyboard, sometimes talking to myself, occasionally storming out over computer glitches. Thank you also to my extended family and friends whose encouragement kept me writing, especially my brother, Keith Kaniut, the very talented writer of the "Agent Eleven" story.

Introduction

National attention on improving math and science test scores in our public schools has left writing curriculum in the dust. Yet it is inconceivable that employers would overlook poor reading and writing skills. Educators know that reading and writing skills improve together. Students must comprehend what they read, process the information, evaluate it critically, and respond to it. The same skills are essential for writing students as well as for math and science students. In fact they are essential in most professional careers. Without communication skills, engineers cannot explain their innovations to manufacturers, medical researchers cannot report their findings, managers cannot lead and motivate their employees, and students cannot improve their proficiency test scores.

Studies have shown that students who play musical instruments do better in math classes. The ability to read musical scores and translate them into the manual dexterity that is required to produce notes from instruments has been scientifically proven to increase the number of electrical synapses in their brains. It is logical to assume that training young students to turn their thoughts and feelings into written words would help their fresh, creative imaginations develop more electrical synapses as well. Both music and writing require the rational thinking skills of the left brain and the intuitive skills of the right brain.

Educators have also known for years that teaching grammar alone does not improve writing skills (Vandeweghe). Rather, writing improves with practice. The best writers begin writing in early grade school and hone their skills through high school. Most writing curriculum revolves around evaluating reading assignments. The trouble is, students have such a wide range of interests and aptitudes in reading that it is difficult to find reading material that grabs their attention. Some may gravitate toward nonfiction such as sports biographies or dinosaur discoveries, while others prefer fiction that is scary, or silly, or a mystery, adventure, or fantasy. Early grade school students are not ready to tackle classic literature together. However, they often enjoy a common familiarity with fairy tales.

This book offers ideas to help teachers energize their writing assignments. Ann Martin (Martin, 4) states that "the sources of writing have to be activated first, before we can impose standards of form." She maintains that we must "respect the complexity of children's thoughts and feelings" before children are taught how to "organize them into written form." In other words, children's imaginations need to be activated or fired up before they are taught grammar and writing style. Students who are given creative writing prompts and exercises like the ones in this book are given permission to think, to explore their own ideas, to make personal decisions, and to express themselves.

By tapping the knowledge students already have of fairy tales, poetry, history, and cultural mythology, teachers will stimulate the imaginations of their students. The creative writing exercises in each chapter teach students how to read a story as a writer and to evaluate the plot, characters, setting, and situation. Students decide what makes the story exciting or scary and consider how making small changes to the original will alter the ending. The process of evaluating stories is a critical writing skill.

Why must these exercises lead to plays? While young students might struggle with reading and writing, their verbal skills are well developed. They know how to get what they want. Their empathic skills are also keen. They know when someone is crabby, silly, sad, or angry. By concentrating on the spoken dialog of a play, they focus on their characters' personalities. They imagine the tone of voice, inflections, and actions of their characters, without being bogged down with dry, descriptive paragraphs. They must "show rather than tell," a writing class mantra, how characters behave and feel through action and dialog.

In his book, *Playmaking,* Daniel Sklar says that while writing their own plays, students "develop language arts skills" (Sklar, ix). At the same time they learn to "appreciate their own feelings and to use their own imaginations" (Sklar, ix). In producing their own plays, they learn "self-discipline, cooperation and mutual respect" (Sklar, ix). Sklar came to this conclusion following a program he led in Macon, Georgia, where students wrote and produced their own plays for their community. "The kids' work emerged as a vital new force in the community" (Sklar, 70). They were empowered by their work. Sklar confirmed the usefulness of plays as a tool to enhance writing programs as well as other classroom skills through his fieldwork. This book presents a simpler version of his twenty-week program, and it is designed for classroom teachers rather than for visiting writing specialists.

When students are asked to give their plays a formal reading, or better yet a performance, they can hear when sentences are unclear, characters do not sound natural, and situations are funny. Plays clearly reveal the power of words as playwrights observe their affect on an audience. All three kinds of learning (the oral, visual, and kinetic learning styles) take place in a play.

This book is a collection of creative writing exercises and original plays, all geared toward students in the third through eighth grades. Language arts, English, history, writing and specials teachers will find *creative* writing ideas as well as material to perform. Teachers choose chapters based on the reading and writing levels of their students. Each chapter introduces a different approach to source material. The beginning chapters are designed for younger students, while the later chapters are for older classes. For instance, a poetry unit can be enhanced with Chapters 1 or 8. Chapter 9 is a great assignment for a history class. The original plays and readers theatre scripts at the end of each chapter are offered as models to inspire new plays. Teachers can decide whether to perform them or merely read them in class.

Each chapter begins with a section titled "Story Adaptation," where source material is suggested. The section explains what questions must be answered to transform the source material into a play. There are worksheets that can be copied and used to organize students' prewriting thoughts. As writers consider their source material and how to adapt it into an original play, they must make decisions and solve problems. Examples demonstrate the process.

In the next section of each chapter, "Playwriting," elements such as the structure of the play, characters, set, costumes, and props are discussed. Some material is better suited to readers theatre while other projects lead to plays. Readers theatre is different from plays in that the performers are not expected to act or memorize their parts. They are given specially bound copies of the script to carry onstage and read. Sometimes costumes are worn but not always. Sets are also minimal, ranging from a few chairs and stools arranged in specific ways to nothing at all on stage. These scripts are a great way to get students used to performing without having to deal with the stage jitters associated with memorization and acting. Students can read in the front of a classroom, without the need for a stage. Such readings are also less time consuming to prepare and perform.

Teachers decide whether each student will write an original version of a story or whether the entire class will generate a single story and script. If each student creates an individual story, a formal reading by a classroom full of "hams" can be turned into a contest. Then only the winning play or top three plays are performed, whether it is for other classes or an auditorium filled with parents.

A contest gives students a target audience, which helps them focus on what is appropriate, and provides a forum for critiques. When students learn how to discuss strengths and weaknesses in their scripts, they not only produce better writing, but they also get a chance to practice diplomacy, critical thinking, and problem solving. Worksheets are provided in this book to help steer these discussions as well. Students learn to phrase their comments in supportive and helpful ways, and teachers must make

Introduction

it clear that the script is under discussion, not the writer. Discussions begin with positive feedback and finish with suggestions for how to strengthen and clarify the work. Writers who welcome such critiques become stronger writers who are able to accept change as a positive thing. A critique can also let writers know that their script is wonderful already and should be submitted for publication immediately.

Ambitious student writers will want to cast and direct their own plays, or they may act as advisors for students who wish to take on those roles. Many schools have special teachers who lead groups for chorale, band, orchestra, art, theater, and even musical performances. These teachers may be willing to assist with a performance. Art teachers can help students create backdrops or props. All of these activities help writers see the fruits of their labor, building enthusiasm for the written word and for improving reading and writing skills.

Before turning to the first chapter, consider trying the following technique to demonstrate the creative possibilities for your students. Canadian author Karleen Bradford introduced me to the concept of clustering (Bradford). Clustering works for a group or an individual. However, when an entire classroom of students tries it, each new idea builds on the last as stories develop, and it is very exciting to watch students inspire each other. Once the concept is demonstrated for the whole class, students are eager to tackle such assignments on their own or in small groups.

Begin by asking the class to suggest a main character—preferably not just a name, but also an occupation such as student, president, or shepherd. After all the suggestions have been written on the board in front of the class, take a blind vote for all the choices, listing the number of votes next to each character. The winner becomes the hero of your story. Erase everything else and draw a circle around your hero. Next, ask students to suggest a location such as London, a barnyard, or the planet Zanuba. Tell the students that the more specific they are, the more material they will have for their story. Repeat the vote-erase-circle process, drawing a line from one circle to the next. The board will look like this.

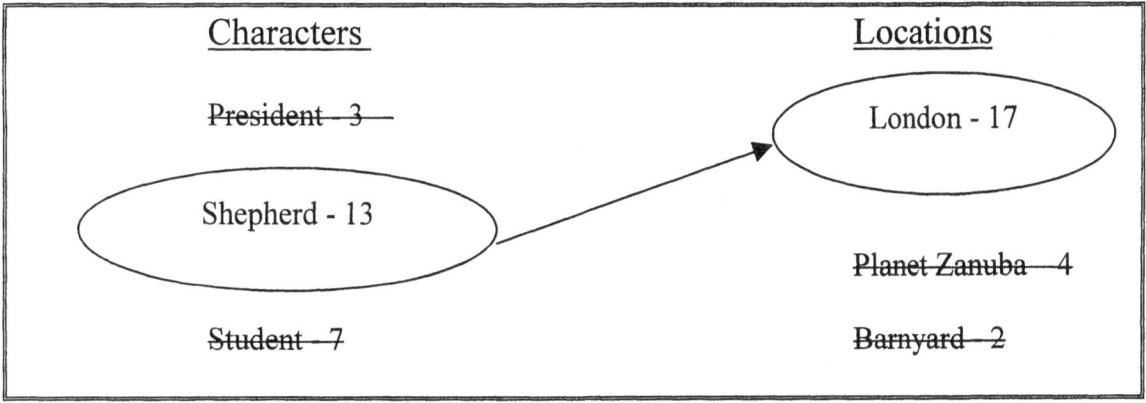

At this point the class needs to come up with a conflict for the hero in this location. Suggest that they keep it simple. Consider the following possibilities:

- Shepherd lost her flock in London.

- Student is kidnapped and taken to the planet Zanuba.

- President only feels safe when surrounded by barnyard animals.

Their decisions become the basis for a simple story, or several stories. Students will have to solve the conflict, describe the places, create support characters, and wrap it all up for a satisfying ending. Older students can continue with a subplot by using the same process. This process may look like the bubble concept used in many classrooms, except here it helps generate choices and then narrows them down to the most interesting one. Bubbles are generally used to help students categorize and list details, while clustering is more like a free association exercise.

Once you've decided whether to attempt a single class story or individual ones, based on the age and writing skills of the group, you are ready to choose a chapter.

To paraphrase one of my favorite characters in Maurice Sendak's *Where the Wild Things Are*, Now let the creative writing begin.

References

Bradford, Karleen. Canadian author and fellow member of the Society of Children's Book Writers and Illustrators. "Re: clustering." E-mail to Lisa Cobb, August 8, 2001.

Martin, Ann. "Allowing the Unconventional," *Educating the Imagination: Essays and Ideas for Teachers and Writers,* ed. Christopher Edgar and Ron Padgett, Vol. 2. New York: Teachers and Writers Collaborative, 1994.

Sklar, Daniel. *Playmaking: Children Writing and Performing Their Own Plays.* New York: Teachers and Writers Collaborative, 1991.

Vandeweghe, Rick. Chairman, Department of English at the University of Colorado at Denver, Chairman of Colorado Writing Project. Personal interview, October 30, 2002.

Additional Reading

Edgar, Christopher and Ron Padgett. *Educating the Imagination, Vol. 2.* New York: Teachers and Writers Collaborative, 1994.

Galt, Margot Fortunato. *The Story in History: Writing Your Way into the American Experience.* New York: Teachers and Writers Collaborative, 1992.

Ray, Katie Wood. *Wondrous Words: Writers and Writing in Elementary Classrooms.* Urbana, IL: National Council of Teachers of English, 2001.

Ray, Katie Wood with Lester L. Laminack. *The Writing Workshop: Working through the Hard Parts.* Urbana, IL: National Council of Teachers of English, 1999.

Tanner, Fran Averett. *Readers Theater: Fundamentals, 2nd Ed.* Topeka, KS: Clark Publishing, Inc. 1993.

1

Poetry for Choral Readings

This chapter demonstrates the creation of two original choral readings. The first one is an adaptation of the E. E. Cummings poem "in Just-." The second choral reading is based on Lewis Carroll's "The Walrus and the Carpenter." Any poem can be adapted. For instance, teachers can choose poems written during the time of their current history unit, or one from the state or country in a geography lesson. Exploring the poetry of a time period or geographic region stimulates student's creative juices, broadening their experience by allowing them to explore beyond the dry facts and into the realm of emotions and sensations.

Unless you choose poetry that is available in the public domain, the issue of copyright infringement may arise. If your students wish to submit their work for publication, this is a consideration. Work that is in the public domain is available for anyone to use and enjoy. Otherwise the author or publisher will need to be contacted for legal permission to derive a new story from their original.

Story Adaptation

I have been granted permission to use a poem by the modern American poet, E. E. Cummings. His style will appeal to younger classes because his poems are free of capital letters and punctuation and full of glee. "in Just-" is a twenty-four-line poem about a balloon seller whose arrival is a harbinger of spring. It will inspire an original choral reading.

The characters in the poem include a balloon seller, two boys named Eddie and Bill, and two girls named Betty and Isbel. The boys shoot marbles and play pirate games, while the girls play hopscotch and jump rope until they hear the whistles of the balloon man. There is lots of action but very little information about the characters. That is where budding playwrights step in. Each character needs a personality that will govern how he or she interacts with the others. The plot of the script is already laid out in the poem.

Playwriting

Even though E. E. Cummings laid out his poem in twenty-four lines, there are only sixty words. A copy of "in Just-" follows. As you take a moment to read it, notice all the white space the poet left on the page. This space creates natural pauses in the flow of words. It sets the pace, slowing it down as the eye covers the white space on the page and speeding it up when the words are bunched together.

in Just-

E. E. Cummings (1894–1962)

1   in just
2   spring   when the world is mud-
3   luscious the little
4   lame balloonman

5   whistles   far   and wee

6   and eddieandbill come
7   running from marbles and
8   piracies and it's
9   spring

10   when the world is puddle-wonderful

11   the queer
12   old balloonman whistles
13   far   and   wee
14   and bettyandisbel come dancing

15   from hop-scotch and jump-rope and

16   it's
17   spring
18   and

19   the

20   goat-footed
21   balloonMan   whistles
22   far
23   and
24   wee

How can that kind of pacing be reproduced in a choral reading? This is a challenge and one worth attempting because it is such an integral part of the poem. It conjures up the pace of a fresh spring day, when a child rushes outside at the first sign of warm weather. His attention is drawn to such wonders as a mud puddle or a game of hopscotch. The goal is to create that same sense of wonder and joy in the script. Pacing will be crucial.

Consider the balloon man. He is little, lame, old and he carries a whistle to let the children know he is coming to their neighborhood. What kind of person would make a living this way? Is he friendly or surly? In our version, the balloon man will be a retired war veteran, which puts the story in a historical frame. It makes sense to set the story between the two world wars because the children are playing old-fashioned games.

Who are Eddie and Bill? The poet writes the characters' names as a single word—eddieandbill—so they must be inseparable friends. They run "from marbles and piracies." This could mean they have just won all the marbles and have a gang of angry boys chasing them because they've cheated at the game. They could also be two young boys who like to pretend and wear newspaper pirate hats while fencing with sticks. Because they like pretend games, we'll make them young. Betty and Isbel play hopscotch and jump rope. Their names are also written as one word—bettyandisbel. Let's make them older and wiser big sisters to the boys. This creates a boy–girl rivalry that will provide good material for the choral reading. Even more tension can be built by making the boys rambunctious and the girls bossy.

With five characters, this could easily become a full play. Since we've decided to create a choral reading for younger classes, we need to add specific characters: a narrator and a chorus. If we look for repetitive elements in the poem, we find "spring," "whistle," and "wee." Put these words together and what do you see? Perhaps they are playful springtime fairies. Perhaps their movements can be fast or slow to mimic the flow of the words. These sprites can be responsible for repeating "wee" where needed.

There are still several things to decide, including costumes, set, and staging. Costumes are simple—play clothes for the children. The balloon seller wears an army helmet because he is a veteran. The boys wear newspaper pirate hats and carry broken tree branches for their pirate swords, perhaps even tucking them into a belt. Since it is "a mud-luscious spring," they will look muddy. The girls wear rubber boots for splashing in puddles.

The set is divided into two areas, a boy territory and a girl territory. The boys have a circle of string surrounding a set of marbles, while the girls have a hopscotch board drawn with chalk, two stones, and a jump rope. The time, place, and characters have already been decided. It is time to listen to what they have to say. The script for *Mudluscious* on the following pages shows one way this poem can be adapted.

MUDLUSCIOUS

Summary

This is play for five characters—two little boys, two little girls, and a little old man—plus a chorus of springtime sprites and a narrator. One day the little old man comes into the neighborhood to sell balloons. The story is based on a poem by E. E. Cummings called "in Just-."

Set

The stage is divided into two territories, one for girls and one for boys. The girls have a hopscotch board drawn in chalk, while the boys have a string circle with a marble collection.

Props

The girls need two stones and chalk for the hopscotch game and a sparkle jump rope. The boys have marbles, a three-foot piece of string tied to create their marble circle, small tree branches (for swords) tucked into oversized belts, and newspaper pirate hats. The old man has red, yellow, blue, purple, green, and pink helium balloons and a whistle.

Costumes

The two girls wear dresses with pinafores and rubber rain boots. The two boys wear cut-off pants, large belts, torn T-shirts, and an eye patch, and they have muddy knees and faces and bare feet. The balloon man wears an old army helmet. The narrator wears stage-reading glasses and carries a copy of the poem to read. The chorus wears spring flower wreaths on their heads or butterfly wings.

Characters

Narrator
Betty
Isbel
Eddie
Bill
Balloon man
Chorus

MUDLUSCIOUS

(Each character walks onstage and introduces her/himself, then takes position indicated.)

Narrator: Hello, my name is _____. I am the narrator. *(Sits cross-legged center stage front.)*

Betty: Hello, my name is _____. I play Betty. *(Plays hopscotch.)*

Isbel: Hello, my name is _____. I play Isbel. *(Jumps rope.)*

Eddie: Hello, my name is _____. I play Eddie. *(Shoots marbles.)*

Bill: Hello, my name is _____. I play Bill. *(Joins Eddie.)*

Balloon man: Hello, my name is _____. I play the balloon man. *(Limps offstage.)*

Chorus: Hello, we are the chorus. Wee! *(Skips offstage.)*

Narrator: *(Clears throat.)* Ahem. *(Puts on reading glasses and reads slowly.)* In . . . Just- . . . spring . . .

Chorus: *(Skips onstage.)* Weeeee!

Narrator: *(Waits for chorus to settle down across the back of the stage.)* When the world is mud *(Pauses.)* luscious . . .

Chorus: Mmmmm. *(Wiggles hands and feet on the floor as if in a mud puddle.)*

Narrator: . . . the little lame balloonman comes . . .

Balloon man: *(Whistles and enters with balloons, limping.)*

> Balloon man coming.
> I've got blues, reds, and yellows
> for all you merry fellows.
> Purple, green, and pink,
> come see what you think. *(Exits.)*

Chorus: *(Doing the wave each time they say this.)* Weeeee!

Narrator: . . . and eddieandbill . . .

Eddie: *(Stands and looks around.)* I heard him, did you?

Bill: Who?

Eddie: The balloon man and his whistle . . . where is he?

Bill: Wait, listen.

Balloon man: *(Whistles offstage.)*

Eddie: Over there—come on. *(Runs a few steps, then stops, looking down.)*

Bill: Ooh, look at the mud.

Eddie: Wow. *(Drops to hands and knees to squish imaginary mud.)* It's perfect.

Chorus: Weeeee!

Narrator: . . . come running from marbles . . .

Eddie: *(Plays in mud.)* Hey, I'll swap my yellow cats eye for your blue one.

Bill: No way, but I'll take your black one for it.

Eddie: Let's shoot for 'em. Best two out of three?

Bill: Deal, but first I want to see the balloons. Where did he go?

Eddie: Listen.

Balloon man: *(Whistles offstage.)*

Chorus: Wee!

Narrator: Uh, let's see . . . from marbles and piracies . . .

Bill: Avast. He's off the starboard bow.

Eddie: Do you mean the right?

Bill: Yeah, starboard.

Eddie: Are you sure?

Bill: He's behind your house. Let's go.

Eddie: Aaargh ye matey, wait for me. *(Both run off stage.)*

Narrator: When the world is puddle- . . . wonderful.

Chorus: Weeeee! *(Kicks feet as if splashing.)*

Narrator: . . . the queer . . .

Balloon man: *(Enters with balloons.)* Get your little rubber bag full of helium, the air that's lighter than air. It's magic. Get your magic air here.

Narrator: . . . old . . .

Balloon man: Get your balloons now, so I don't have to carry them around any more. Come on kids, give an old guy a break.

Narrator: . . . the old balloonman . . . *(Plugs ears with fingers.)*

Balloon man: *(Whistles.)*

Narrator: . . . whistles . . . far and . . .

Chorus: Weeeee!

Narrator: . . . and bettyandisbel come dancing . . .

Betty: *(Stands and skips.)*

Isbel: *(Hooks elbows with Betty and swings like a square dance.)* Swing your partner round and round, now . . .

Betty: Now we're ballerinas. *(Twirls on tiptoe.)*

Isbel: *(Twirls.)*

Narrator: . . . from hop-scotch . . .

Betty: Did you bring our stones? I don't want to lose mine.

Isbel: Yeah, I know. It took us forever to find these.

Narrator: . . . and jump-rope . . .

Betty: Uh, oh. Where's my new sparkle jump rope?

Isbel: Right here, Betty. You forget everything.

Narrator: It's spring . . .

Chorus: Weeeee!

Narrator: . . . and . . . the . . . goat-footed . . .

Balloon man: Who are you calling goat-footed? What do you mean by that?

Narrator: That means sure-footed. You jump, climb, hop, sprint, and never fall.

Balloon man: Who are you kidding? I haven't jumped for years, not to mention hopped or sprinted. I'm old and lame, remember?

Narrator: Right. Maybe the children were goat-footed.

Balloon man: Sure, that makes more sense. I mean, just look at them.

(Enter Eddie and Bill, who join Betty and Isbel as they dance in a circle.)

Narrator: Right. Now where was I? Oh yes, the balloonMan . . . *(Fingers in ears.)*

Balloon man: *(Whistles.)*

Narrator: . . . whistles far and . . .

Chorus: Weeeee!

Narrator: The end.

Chorus: Not yet, we want to dance too. *(Joins children in circle.)*

Narrator: Oh all right, go ahead. Ahem. Not yet the end.

Chorus: *(Leaves circle.)* Weeeee! *(Bows.)*

Narrator: Now?

Chorus: Yes.

Narrator: The end. *(Children stop, bow with Narrator and chorus.)*

Balloon man: *(Blows whistle.)* What about me?

Chorus: Come on. *(Waves him into their line. All bow and skip off stage, except Balloon man, who limps.)*

Note: The following credit line must be included in all program materials used in conjunction with performances of this play. If paid performances are contemplated, permission must be obtained directly from Liveright Publishing Corporation.

CREDIT LINE: "in Just-." Copyright 1923, 1951, © 1991 by the Trustees for the E. E. Cummings Trust. Copyright © 1976 by George James Firmage, from COMPLETE POEMS: 1904–1962 by E. E. Cummings, edited by George J. Firmage. Used by permission of Liveright Publishing Corporation.

Story Adaptation

Another well-known author, Lewis Carroll, wrote a long, silly poem called "The Walrus and the Carpenter," which is in the public domain. Students may recognize the poem's style from Carroll's famous book, *Alice in Wonderland*. "The Walrus and the Carpenter" tells of an unlikely pair of friends out walking on a beach on a fine night who invite some oysters to join them. Can you picture anything sillier? Lewis Carroll can. The older and wiser oysters decline the offer, but soon the two friends are followed by a long line of young oysters. For our play they will become the chorus. Seven maids with seven mops as well as a sulky moon and an over-eager sun round out the cast. This poem is 108 lines long and is written in rhyme with a measured, singsong beat. It will be fun to try to preserve as much of that as possible. Lewis Carroll's dialog shows that the walrus and carpenter are a couple of emotional fellows, two silly characters in a silly setting. What a great place to start.

Playwriting

The first exercise in this chapter was short and a simple adaptation. Let's see how this can work for a longer poem. Take a moment to read Lewis Carroll's poem "The Walrus and the Carpenter," reprinted below. Better yet, close the door and read it out loud, and as you do, listen to the pacing and rhyme. Does your head start wagging from side to side with the rhythm? Do you develop a kind of carefree and playful voice?

The Walrus and the Carpenter

Lewis Carroll (1832–1898)

1 The sun was shining on the sea,
2 Shining with all his might:
3 He did his very best to make
4 The billows smooth and bright—
5 And this was odd, because it was
6 The middle of the night.

7 The moon was shining sulkily,
8 Because she thought the sun
9 Had got no business to be there
10 After the day was done—
11 'It's very rude of him,' she said,
12 'To come and spoil the fun.'

13 The sea was wet as wet could be,
14 The sands were dry as dry.
15 You could not see a cloud, because
16 No cloud was in the sky:
17 No birds were flying overhead—
18 There were no birds to fly.

19 The Walrus and the Carpenter
20 Were walking close at hand;
21 They wept like anything to see

22 Such quantities of sand:
23 'If this were only cleared away,'
24 They said, 'it would be grand!'

25 'If seven maids with seven mops
26 Swept it for half a year,
27 Do you suppose,' the Walrus said,
28 'That they could get it clear?'
29 'I doubt it,' said the Carpenter,
30 And shed a bitter tear.

31 'O Oysters, come and walk with us!'
32 The Walrus did beseech.
33 'A pleasant walk, a pleasant talk,
34 Along the briny beach:
35 We cannot do with more than four,
36 To give a hand to each.'

37 The eldest Oyster looked at him,
38 But never a word he said:
39 The eldest Oyster winked his eye,
40 And shook his heavy head—
41 Meaning to say he did not choose
42 To leave the oyster-bed.

43 But four young Oysters hurried up,
44 All eager for the treat:
45 Their coats were brushed, their faces washed,
46 Their shows were clean and neat—
47 And this was odd, because, you know,
48 They hadn't any feet.

49 Four other Oysters followed them,
50 And yet another four;
51 And thick and fast they came at last,
52 And more, and more, and more—
53 All hopping through the frothy waves,
54 And scrambling to the shore.

55 The Walrus and the Carpenter
56 Walked on a mile or so,
57 And then they rested on a rock
58 Conveniently low:
59 And all the little Oysters stood
60 And waited in a row.

61 'The time has come,' the Walrus said,
62 'To talk of many things:
63 Of shoes—and ships—and sealing-wax—
64 Of cabbages—and kings—
65 And why the sea is boiling hot—
66 And whether pigs have wings.'

67 'But wait a bit,' the Oysters cried,
68 'Before we have our chat;
69 For some of us are out of breath,
70 And all of us are fat!'
71 'No hurry!' said the Carpenter.
72 They thanked him much for that.

73 'A loaf of bread,' the Walrus said,
74 'Is what we chiefly need:
75 Pepper and vinegar besides
76 Are very good indeed—
77 Now if you're ready, Oysters dear,
78 We can begin to feed.'

79 'But not on us!' the Oysters cried,
80 Turning a little blue.
81 'After such kindness, that would be
82 A dismal thing to do!'
83 'The night is fine,' the Walrus said.
84 'Do you admire the view?

85 'It was so kind of you to come!
86 And you are very nice!'
87 The Carpenter said nothing but
88 'Cut us another slice:
89 I wish you were not quite so deaf—
90 I've had to ask you twice!'

91 'It seems a shame,' the Walrus said,
92 'To play them such a trick,
93 After we've brought them out so far,
94 And made them trot so quick!'
95 The Carpenter said nothing but
96 'The butter's spread too thick!'

97 'I weep for you,' the Walrus said:
98 'I deeply sympathize.'
99 With sobs and tears he sorted out
100 Those of the largest size,
101 Holding his pocket-handkerchief
102 Before his streaming eyes.

103 'O Oysters,' said the Carpenter,
104 'You've had a pleasant run!
105 Shall we be trotting home again?'
106 But answer came there none—
107 And this was scarcely odd, because
108 They'd eaten every one.

Carroll has created a lighthearted romp and that is what we will also try to achieve with our choral reading.

To convert this poem to a choral reading, we start with the characters. The oysters will be the chorus while the other characters have walk-on parts. A narrator is needed to describe how the sun shines and the moon sulks, or we could make them characters as well. A narrator must still introduce the walrus and the carpenter, who then begin a dialog. As the story unfolds, the narrator can explain parts that cannot be made into dialog.

Costumes will help tell this story. The carpenter needs a tool belt with a hammer, the walrus should wear a brown oversized man's suit and a long, white fake mustache combed into two definite points in place of tusks. A trip to the thrift shop will turn up a suit if there are no dads willing to lend one. The maids carry mops and wear aprons, the sulky moon wears white from head to toe, and the sun wears all yellow. The oysters are a challenge. The simplest solution is to make matching hats out of one white paper plate for each person in the oyster chorus. The plate is cut in the middle so that one half is tied on the head like a headband, while the other half becomes a necklace. The heads of the chorus appear to be sandwiched between the two plate halves. Another option is to create clam-shaped hats out of two white paper plates and tie them on with a piece of yarn or elastic that goes under the chin. The oysters' clothes should match. Keep it simple with something like blue jeans and white T-shirts.

A long piece of blue cloth laid out along the front of the stage will be the ocean. This cloth is held at both ends by "stage hands," wearing all blue and making the cloth flutter like waves. A "conveniently low" rock is made from a low bench or box draped with tan burlap. The characters will march around the stage like a conga line, marching to the beat of the poem, with the carpenter and walrus in the lead. The only question remaining is how to make the oysters disappear as they are eaten. The walrus sorts them and the carpenter doesn't notice they are gone, so his back must be to the oysters while he is sitting on his rock. Perhaps the waves can wash up, billowing high so the oysters can sneak or perhaps roll away near the end of the script. Let's call this script something silly like *The Sunny Night*.

THE SUNNY NIGHT

Summary

A carpenter and a walrus walk on a beach and invite the oysters to join them. The sun shines at night and makes the moon sulky. Silly oysters are in for more than a stroll on the beach. There are a minimum of nineteen parts in this choral reading, although extra players can be added to the oyster chorus.

Set

A low bench covered with "sand-colored" burlap, a length of blue cloth to be the sea.

Props

Seven maids need seven mops. A loaf of bread, a plastic knife, a bottle marked "vinegar," a pepper grinder, and a large handkerchief are all stored in Walrus' pockets.

Costumes

The carpenter wears a tool belt with a hammer stuck in it. The walrus wears an oversized brown suit and a long, white fake mustache combed into two long points to look like tusks. Seven maids wear aprons. The sun wears all yellow; the moon wears all white. The little oysters wear white paper plates on their heads, with paper plate collars; the eldest oyster wears large paper platters the same way.

Characters

Walrus
Carpenter
The Sun
The Moon
Seven Maids
Six Little Oysters
Eldest Oyster
Narrator
Ocean Waves

THE SUNNY NIGHT

(All characters walk onstage, introduce themselves, then exit, except for the stage hands, the eldest oyster, and the sun.)

Walrus: My name is _____. I play the Walrus.

Carpenter: My name is _____. I play the Carpenter.

The Sun: My name is _____. I play the sun.

The Moon: My name is _____. I play the moon.

Seven Maids: We are _____, _____, _____, _____, _____, _____, and _____. We play the seven maids.

Six Little Oysters: We are _____, _____, _____, _____, _____, and _____. We play the little oysters.

Eldest Oyster: My name is _____. I play the eldest oyster.

Narrator: My name is _____. I play the narrator.

Two Ocean Waves: We are _____ and _____. We make the ocean flow.

(The stage hands are in place, moving the "water," and so is Eldest Oyster. Enter the sun.)

Sun: *(Stands with arms akimbo, legs apart.)* The sun, that's me, was shining on the sea, shining with all my might. I did my very best to make the billows smooth and bright— *(Bends and tries to smooth the waves. Stage hands don't cooperate.)*

Narrator: *(Enters.)* And this was odd, because it was the middle of the night.

Moon: *(Enters, crosses arms, and frowns.)* The moon, that's me, was shining sulkily, because I thought the sun had got no business to be there after the day was done. It's very rude of him, I said, to come and spoil the fun.

Narrator: The sea was wet as wet could be, the sands were dry as dry. You could not see a cloud.

Sun: No cloud was in the sky.

Narrator: No birds were flying overhead.

Moon: There were no birds to fly.

Narrator: The walrus and the carpenter were walking close at hand. *(Enter Walrus and Carpenter, bawling loudly.)* They wept like anything to see such quantities of sand.

Carpenter: If this were only cleared away, oh, it would be so grand. *(Enter maids who start to mop.)*

Walrus: If seven maids with seven mops swept it for half a year, do you suppose that they could ever really get it clear?

Carpenter: *(Bawling loudly.)* I doubt it. *(Maids leave disgusted.)*

Walrus: Oh Oysters, come and walk with us, I really do beseech. A pleasant walk and a pleasant talk, along the briny beach.

Carpenter: We cannot do with more than four to give a hand to each. *(Eldest oyster shakes his head slowly "no," then winks, but doesn't move.)*

Walrus: I think he does not choose to leave his cozy oyster bed. *(One young oyster rolls in.)*

Narrator: But one young oyster hurried up, all eager for the treat.

Oyster 1: I brushed my coat, washed my face, and now I'm clean and neat.

Narrator: And this was odd, because, you know, he hadn't any feet. *(Oyster looks up and shrugs.)*

Narrator: Soon other oysters followed him and yet another did; and thick and fast they came at last, and more and more and more—all hopping through the frothy waves and scrambling to the shore. *(Last two oysters roll in.)* The walrus and the carpenter walked on a mile or so, and then they rested on a rock conven—i—ently low, while all the oysters stood, and waited in a row.

Walrus: The time has come to talk of many things: of shoes . . . and ships . . . and sealing wax . . . of cabbages . . . and kings.

Carpenter: *(Sits on the rock, back to Walrus.)* And why the sea is boiling hot and whether pigs have wings.

Oyster 1: But wait a bit,

Oyster 2: Before we have our chat.

Oyster 3: For some of us are out of breath,

Oyster 4: And all of us are fat.

Carpenter: No hurry.

Oysters: *(Together.)* Thank you. *(Oysters sit.)*

Walrus: *(Reaches into pockets.)* A loaf of bread is what we chiefly need,

Carpenter: Pepper and vinegar besides, oh good show old man.

Walrus: Now if you're ready, Oysters dear, we can begin to feed . . .

Oysters: *(Together.)* But not on us!

Narrator: They turned a little blue.

Carpenter: *(Quietly.)* Cut me another slice.

Oyster 1: After such kindness

Oyster 2: That would be . . .

Oyster 3: A dismal thing to do!

Walrus: The night is fine. Take a look. Do you admire the view? *(Points first oyster toward the sea then scoops him into jacket. Fabric "waves" high as oyster slips away, hat visible on top of "water." Walrus turns back around and licks his fingers.) (Inspects second oyster.)* You are very nice.

Carpenter: *(Sits with back to walrus.)* Cut us another slice! I wish you were not quite so deaf—I've had to ask you twice!

Walrus: *(Spreads imaginary butter over a slice of bread.)* It seems a shame to play them such a trick, after we've brought them out so far, and made them trot so quick.

Carpenter: *(Inspects bread and waves it over shoulder, angry.)* The butter's spread too thick!

Walrus: *(Sorts oysters, one rolls away.)* I weep for you. I deeply sympathize. *(Bawls and wipes eyes with large handkerchief.)*

Carpenter: Oh oysters, you've had a pleasant run. Shall we be trotting home again? *(Turns to look at Walrus and the oysters. Shows surprise.)*

Narrator: But answer came there none, and this was scarcely odd, because he'd eaten every one. *(Bows and leaves.)*

Carpenter and Walrus: *(Bawl loudly and exit. Sun and moon stalk off.)*

Eldest Oyster: The End.

Other Poems to Adapt

Choral readings have plenty of parts for a classroom full of eager actors. Again, if your plays will be performed for a paying audience, remember to check the copyright status of the poems. Children's librarians in public libraries can steer you toward collections of poetry, however, the best source of poetry can be the students. The exercise in this chapter can follow a poetry unit for any grade level. If poetry is not part of the year's curriculum, perhaps an older class that just finished their poetry unit would allow their work to inspire younger students. They might even agree to be an audience for the young playwrights.

Extensions

1. Ask for volunteers to choose music to accompany your choral reading. *Mudluscious* would be fun with some square dance music, something adventurous for the pirates, and something graceful for the ballerinas. Students would choose the music and then learn a few bars to play at the appropriate time in the reading. Even beginning band students can tackle this assignment with a little guidance from their band teacher.

2. Have students make fairy wings or spring flower hair wreathes for the *Mudluscious* chorus, and the paper-plate oyster hats for the chorus in *The Sunny Night*.

3. Assign a student prop master to get the balloons and whistle for *Mudluscious*, or all of Walrus' cooking supplies and the cloth for the sea needed in *The Sunny Night*.

2

Fairy Tales for Readers Theatre

Story Adaptation

I once asked a class to list their favorite fairy tales and they came up with forty titles, so you might want to give students a time limit or some other limiting factor if you're planning to cluster this exercise. A show of hands can determine which tales are unfamiliar to the majority of students. Eliminate those in order to avoid the need to explain the story before beginning the adaptation.

Adapting a story for readers theatre is similar to that of choral readings, but there are some key differences. First, you usually won't have a chorus to echo lines and play pranks. Second, actors don't memorize their lines but read them from a script, which they carry onstage. Hence the name readers theatre. Third, the actors don't usually have to act. They hold their scripts and sit or stand, facing the audience. Costumes, props, and stage sets are nonexistent or minimal. The idea is to draw in the audience members, making them feel like they are a part of the performance through the oral delivery.

Staging is innovative and very different from a regular play. Lines spoken to other characters in the script are read by an actor facing the audience. Stage stools or chairs face the audience. For example, a readers theatre version of the scene between Adam and Eve by the apple tree would have Eve sitting in a chair holding her script. She would read her line, "Come on, Adam. Try the apple. You'll like it." Then she would look up and hold out an empty palm to the audience as if offering the imaginary apple to them. Adam would respond by looking at the audience in puzzlement, then reach toward them and pretend he's taking an apple. He might mime taking a bite before saying, "Mmmm, sure, but that's not the point, is it?"

Readers theatre is similar to choral readings because the story is told through characters and their dialog. The story happens through what the characters say. Taking a familiar tale and retelling it this way allows students to consider the story and action from another viewpoint. What motivates the characters, what are they afraid of, how will they get out of their mess? Students must solve problems and sympathize with the feelings of others, exercises that are always welcome in a classroom.

Most students already like "what if" games, like "What if you were the richest person in the world. What would you do?" or "What if you had three wishes." A playwright has to climb into a character's head and think, "What if I were Cinderella. Would I go to the ball?" Cinderella goes, but what if she is way too shy to be comfortable and excited about it? What if she would really rather curl up with a good book and a cup of tea? What convinces Cinderella to go? There's the conflict and the emotional response that creates a spark for a reader or audience.

The other big similarity is that choral readings and readers theatre both have narrators. The writer or adaptor decides how big or small this part is in the story. In *Mudluscious,* the narrator was the glue that stuck all the images together, creating a brief moment in time with a story that appeared to flow like a river, moving things along. Sometimes the narrator tells crucial information, like descriptions of places or time in a story. Sometimes the narrator simply gets things started and then wraps things up in the end.

Playwriting

In this chapter we will adapt the story of "The Three Billy Goats Gruff" to a readers theatre script. The title points to three characters—the goats. The story's conflict is created by the troll under the bridge. A narrator could explain where they are and introduce the characters. That would make five parts for this script.

There is no need to build a bridge for the troll in readers theatre format, but staging can create the illusion of one. If the troll sits on the floor, while the goats sit on high stools, the impression the goats are overhead is achieved. Sound affects can enhance the experience of readers theatre as well. The sound of goat hooves on a wooden bridge are implied by "the goats" tapping their stools with a wooden spoon at the appropriate moment.

To ensure that the audience knows who is speaking, have the students use appropriate voices. The troll speaks gruffly, with a gravely voice. The youngest billy goat has a high, squeaky voice, the middle one has a normal voice, while the oldest billy goat has a deep, low voice. In addition, it is customary to have readers introduce themselves at the beginning so that there is no confusion.

When considering how to start the play, remember that most fairy tales begin with the phrase "Once upon a time." This is how our narrator will get things started for us. The trick is to decide what tone to set. Is the narrator part of the story or an outsider who is watching the play like the audience? The two narrators in Chapter 1 were this kind of outsider. They created a bridge between the characters and the audience. Wouldn't it be interesting to have the troll be our narrator for this script? What a great way to involve the audience in the story, because the narrator would be that connection, that bridge between the goats and the audience. This familiar story can be explored through the troll's eyes because the narrator is allowed to make comments directly to the audience, ensuring that his viewpoint and opinions about the actions are what the audience understands. This also reduces the number of characters to only four.

Imagine the troll lumbering onto the stage and then sitting cross-legged in front of the three stools before he addresses the audience. The "goats" can be seated already, waiting for their cues. This avoids having each goat walk on and tell his part individually. It will be much more interesting if they engage in a conversation. Since our viewpoint is shifted to the troll, the title can reflect his feelings. We'll call this script *The Last Toll*.

THE LAST TOLL

Summary

A troll tells the story of the day he thought he would try to be nice, for once. That was the day three billy goat brothers tricked him out of eating them. That was the first and last time he ever went to sleep hungry. This is a readers theatre script for four characters.

Set

Three bar stools are arranged in the center of the stage, with space in the front for the troll to sit on the floor.

Props

Three wooden spoons are waiting on the stools.

Costumes

No costumes are required.

Characters

Max
Frank
Willie
Crunch

THE LAST TOLL

Max: *(Enters and sits on a stool. Speaks with a deep voice.)* Hello, my name is _____. I play the oldest billy goat who is named Max.

Frank: *(Enters and sits. Uses a normal voice.)* Hi, my name is _____. I play the middle billy goat named Frank.

Willie: *(Enters and sits. Uses a squeaky high voice.)* Hi, my name is _____. I play the youngest billy goat named Willie.

Crunch: *(Enters and sits cross-legged on the floor. Speaks with a gravelly voice.)* Hi, my name is _____. I play the troll named Crunch and I am also the narrator. Ready guys?

Goats: *(Together, getting comfortable on their seats.)* Yep.

Crunch: Once upon a time, I used to live under a bridge. It crossed a river between two fields of grass.

Max: There were lots of animals on our side of the bridge.

Frank: The deer always ate more than their share.

Willie: And I was always hungry.

Crunch: So one day these goats decided to just trot across my bridge and eat the grass on the other side.

Max: We were doing a scientific test. We wanted to see if the grass really *is* always greener on the other side.

Crunch: They totally disregarded all the signs that I posted.

Frank: We saw the signs, they said "Troll Bridge." We thought someone was a very bad speller.

Willie: I couldn't read at that time, so it wasn't my fault.

Max: We thought someone had put the "r" in there just to be silly.

Crunch: Oh, right, it must have been the hyena that tried to cross the day before you did. By the time I finished with him, I forgot to change the sign before you arrived. Do you want to know why the grass is always greener on the other side?

Max: That was the idea, Crunch. We were going to cross the bridge and find out why.

Crunch: Well, it's greener because of the toll bridge. You have to pay the price for that greener grass, and since most folks can't pay, it stays greener. I suppose you couldn't read the part on the signs that said a toll must be paid?

Frank: Sure we could, but like I said, we thought it was a joke.

Crunch: Are you calling the way I made my living a joke?

Frank: Absolutely and positively not. No, I would never say that. I would never even imply that, Crunch. I just meant . . .

Crunch: Well, it wasn't a joke. It's a very well-known traditional job for trolls, to be bridge keepers, that is. My grandfather and his grandfather and his grandfather before him were all toll bridge keepers.

Willie: *(Giggles.)* It sounded like you said troll.

Crunch: Well I didn't.

Frank: Don't get him riled up, Willie. He always gets testy when he tells this story.

Max: I'd like to take this opportunity to point out that we would have paid a toll if we'd known about it.

Crunch: Oh, really? Ignorance is no excuse. Are you saying you would have been happy to pay the tax?

Max: Is any one ever happy to pay a tax? I mean, when you get right down to it, nobody is ever happy to pay taxes.

Willie: If you don't pay for your taxis, you can get arrested, can't you?

Frank: He said *taxes,* not taxis. One is a payment; the other is a car that takes you places for money.

Willie: Oh. Never mind.

Crunch: I'll bet you still have no idea what that tax is, do you?

Frank: No, Crunch, we don't know what it is. I assumed that was why you called us here today, so you could explain it for us, and collect it.

Willie: You're riling him up, Frank. Cut it out.

Frank: I'm just asking him to get to the point. I'm getting hungry again.

Max: Just so we're clear, before you get started with the story, was it a tax or a toll?

Crunch: Toll, tax, what's the difference? There was a payment due and you never paid it.

Max: Right, okay. Well then, let's get on with the story, shall we?

Crunch: So there I was, napping in the shade under my bridge, waiting for my first customer of the day, when along comes this silly little billy goat, clomping across my bridge like it was some kind of interstate highway.

Willie: *(Taps spoon on chair.)* I just got finished convincing my big brothers to let me go first because I eat so little. If one of them went first, by the time the others got across there might not be any grass left. I was feeling pretty proud of myself.

Crunch: Well I rolled to my feet and started climbing the steep bank of the river up to the top of the bridge. In the meantime I spoke my usual troll greeting.

Frank: You call that roar a greeting? I could hear it all the way back on the other side and it didn't sound friendly at all. It made the grass quake and the trees shake. It sounded like a threat.

Max: Right, a threat. It sounded like a threat to me, too.

Crunch: All I said was, "Who's that trotting across my bridge?" I was just asking who he was.

Willie: Well, I've never been so frightened. There I was all by myself for maybe the first time in my life, feeling all proud one minute and all shivery the next.

Crunch: Aw gee. I didn't mean to scare you, little guy. I was just doing my job.

Willie: That's okay. Don't worry about it. We're friends now, right?

Crunch: Friends? Um, I don't think so. I think I'm still mad at you guys for not paying the toll. Anyway, where was I? Oh, yeah, climbing up the steep bank of the river, which was more slippery than usual due to a rain the night before.

Frank: I remember that now. That was no rain. That was a banging, smashing, crashing, flashing, loud, pouring-down-rain-for-hours storm.

Willie: The bridge was slippery, too.

Crunch: I caught up to you just before you reached the other side and I asked you to please pay the toll.

Willie: If that's how you ask, GIVE ME MY TOLL, then I'm not even a little interested in hearing you demand something.

Crunch: And what did this little scrappy billy goat say? *(Changes voice to squeaky.)* "Oh, please don't eat me. My brother is right behind me and he's much bigger and meatier than I am."

Willie: Did not!

Frank: Did too. I heard you.

Willie: Well I was just joking.

Crunch: You fellas have an interesting sense of humor. Well, I didn't just fall off a turnip truck, and believe you me, I've heard plenty of excuses in my day, so I was prepared. I told the little guy he'd make a fine appetizer.

Willie: I almost fell off the bridge, I was shaking so hard.

Frank: What did you say to that?

Willie: I told him I might spoil his appetite.

Crunch: He had a good point and it was a clever answer, so I figured I got partial payment. Anyway I let him pass. I was powerful hungry and knew I could eat a much bigger goat if I could just wait a little longer.

Frank: It was my turn and I heard what they said, so I had a plan. I crossed the bridge and told the troll about Max.

Crunch: Here was a good-sized billy goat standing there and telling me there was an even bigger goat coming along right behind him. My mouth started watering just thinking about it.

Frank: I'll say it did. In fact, you started drooling all over the bridge and I had to jump over a puddle the size of the Pacific Ocean.

Max: Don't exaggerate, Frank. It always gets you in trouble.

Frank: Not that time, it didn't. I told him you were the size of Paul Bunyon's ox, Big Blue, and he believed me.

Max: I am not that big. I have big bones.

Crunch: You're not as big as Big Blue. I've met him and he makes me feel like a midget. Well, I let Frank pass as well, even though his story was only a slight variation of Willie's story. It was nevertheless a story and I can't be choosey; it's not in the rules.

Max: Are you telling me there are rules about how you collect tolls?

Crunch: Of course there are, I'm not an ogre. They have no rules, but trolls are much more civilized. I think it was my fiftieth grandfather, Smash, who started the whole story rule. If there was no money to pay the toll, a story would do. He may have had higher standards or maybe he was just bored, but these days the only standard is that it be original.

Max: Amazing. What happens if there is no story and no money?

Crunch: I get to eat you; it's one of the perks of the job. You wouldn't believe, after all these years of toll bridges, how many people try to cross without paying up.

Frank: Maybe that explains the reputation trolls have.

Crunch: What reputation would that be?

Frank: The one about you all being blood-thirsty monsters who eat anyone you can catch.

Crunch: Now that's so unfair. If it were a matter of catching you, I'd starve because I'm not very fast. No, it's just a job. I'll admit that there may be some conspiracy to keep the rules quiet.

Willie: Why would you want to do that?

Crunch: I eat better when people don't know the rules.

Frank: You may be slow, but you're not dumb.

Crunch: Thank you. Now where was I in the story? Oh, yes, I was ready to tell about the part where Max crossed the bridge.

Max: May I?

Crunch: Be my guest.

Max: Well, I knew about the rules, but I'm not much for stories. I figured this troll wasn't too picky if he let Frank and Willie pass. They're not very good at stories either.

Frank: Hey, I resent that.

Max: Nevertheless, *(Taps stool with spoon.)* I started walking when the troll yelled across the bridge.

Crunch: You fellas are so sensitive. I wasn't yelling, merely asking for my toll.

Willie: There's that asking part again—WHERE'S MY TOLL?

Max: I stopped in my tracks and considered the options. My mind went blank, so I knew a story was out of the question. I couldn't even remember my name.

Willie: It's Max.

Max: I know that now, silly. I guess I just acted on instinct. I put my head down and built up some speed.

Crunch: Have you ever stood in front of a freight train that's going full speed? That's what it felt like. The bridge vibrated so much I almost lost my balance. That's probably why I didn't have a chance to swing up onto the railings; I was off balance.

Max: Whatever you say, Crunch. You like to swing onto the railings? That I'd like to see. Anyway, I knocked you so hard you did a back flip.

Crunch: I meant to do that.

Max: Did you mean to land in the river?

Crunch: Sure, but my swan dive was messed up because I had lost my balance.

Frank: Now that's a tall tale if I ever heard one.

Max: Anyway, the bridge was clear, so I headed across and into that nice field of fresh grass and wildflowers. It sure was delicious.

Crunch: That was the day I decided to retire. When my swan dive failed and I did a belly flop into that river full of icy snowmelt from the mountains, I figured I was getting too old for the job. I offered my services to these billy goats. I always dreamed of sitting around a campfire at night and telling all those stories I've been hearing over the years to my friends.

Willie: You tell much better stories than Max does.

Frank: What about me? Aren't my stories original and exciting?

Willie: Sure, but they're all about goats. Crunch tells stories about everyone, everyone who ever crossed his bridge.

Crunch: I never thought of it that way, Willie.

Willie: Well, it's true. Your stories are great, even the ones that I fall asleep during.

Frank: Did I just hear Crunch call us his friends?

Max: That's what it sounded like to me.

Frank: What's that part about campfires, though? We can't do that—no matches, no wood, and no hands make it impossible.

Crunch: It was just a figure of speech, a colorful image.

Willie: You mean, more colorful than the image of the four of us huddled behind a rock, out of the wind, while you tell us stories?

Crunch: Trolls don't huddle.

Max: You don't have to with a thick coat of fur like you have.

Willie: I know I like it when you wrap your arms around me like a blanket. I feel all warm and cozy.

Crunch: Now why did you have to bring that up? Can't a troll save one shred of dignity around you boys? If my family knew I was hanging around with three billy goats, they'd have my hide.

Willie: Then I'd get awfully cold.

Crunch: Let's not talk about huddling out of the wind, but rather about how I serve as your body guard. The stories can be our little secret, okay?

Frank: Is that what you tell everyone? Maybe that explains why no one else has crossed that bridge.

Crunch: That's my story and I'm sticking with it.

Willie: Speaking of stories, it's almost dark so it's time for our story now.

Crunch: What do you think that was? As I said, that's my story, and now this is . . . the end.

(All close scripts, stand, and bow.)

Other Sources

The two books listed below are recommended for further reading. Fran Averett Tanner's book gives information on how to stage readers theatre productions.

Barchers, Suzanne. *Multicultural Folktales: Readers Theatre for Elementary Students.* Englewood, CO: Teacher Ideas Press, 2000.

Tanner, Fran Averett. *Readers Theater: Fundamentals, 2nd Ed.* Topeka, KS: Clark Publishing, Inc., 1993.

There are many books published on writing workshops for students. Three that are particularly appropriate for elementary school classrooms are listed below. Daniel Sklar's book contains discussion on the benefits of children writing and acting in their own plays.

Martin, Ann, "Allowing the Unconventional," *Educating the Imagination: Essays and Ideas for Teachers and Writers,* ed. Christopher Edgar and Ron Padgett, Vol. 2. New York: Teachers and Writers Collaborative, 1994.

Ray, Katie Wood. *Wondrous Words: Writers and Writing in Elementary Classrooms.* Urbana, IL: National Council of Teachers of English, 2001.

Ray, Katie Wood with Lester L. Laminack. *The Writing Workshop: Working through the Hard Parts.* Urbana, IL: National Council of Teachers of English, 1999.

Sklar, Daniel. *Playmaking: Children Writing and Performing Their Own Plays.* New York: Teachers and Writers Collaborative, 1991.

Sloyer, Shirlee. *From the Page to the Stage: The Educator's Complete Guide to Reader's Theater.* Westport, CT: Teacher Ideas Press/Libraries Unlimited, 2003.

3

Fairy Tale Plays

Two plays are created in this chapter to provide a thorough demonstration of how to adapt a familiar story into a play. These exercises allow students to explore stories from a new perspective. Once students learn how to make the adjustment, the same technique will also help them better understand literature and history.

Assume these plays will be staged by third to eighth graders and set down some ground rules. For instance, suggest they figure out how to stage the play in their own school. Are there a stage, curtain, and lights? Or advise students that they must produce their play with no budget, so they will need volunteer actors, borrowed sets, and costumes. Such limitations force students to be creative with found things.

Story Adaptation

Before a play can be written, a story must be analyzed for its theme, setting, characters, and action. Knowing the story's theme helps the playwright stay focused on what must be included in the play. Scenes may need to be cut because of the expense or space, or because they are so brief that it would be simpler to cover their role in the plot through a conversation, which is the crux of a play. Some characters may have to be dropped while others may need to be added in order to clarify action. All of this becomes prewriting notes for the new script. The worksheet at the end of this chapter can be copied and used for planning.

Playwriting

First, lets adapt the story of "Jack and the Beanstalk." Have them analyze the fairy tale for theme—this alone may be an eye-opener, as they discover weighty themes and morals in their favorite stories. What is the theme in "Jack and the Beanstalk"? Is it the obvious—crime doesn't pay? Is it about fair trade? Is there a lesson about how outsiders (giants) are treated? Have the small groups write a short paragraph to describe the theme of the story. When students are able to write a concise sentence about the theme, it helps them focus the action in the story or play.

Next, the students must decide whether they want to set their story in modern times. This decision will affect their sets, costumes, and the language and actions of their characters. Just because Jack believes in magic and giants doesn't mean the play cannot be staged in modern times.

Once the time period is known, the sets can be designed. Take a tour of your school's theater or auditorium. Make a list of all the things you will have at your disposal for staging, such as the availability of a curtain, lights, and sound equipment. Some schools use their gymnasium and install a raised stage. Folding chairs hold the audience. These chairs can be arranged to allow space for actors to move from the stage and through the audience. Have students keep this in mind as they write the action of their plays.

Now read the story and list the locations that are described in it. Jack moves from his farmhouse to the road, into his back yard and up a beanstalk, then into a giant's castle, and back again. That's a lot of sets. Jack's farmhouse can be eliminated if the characters speak in front of their house. A bench and a flowerpot will be enough to indicate the characters are in front of their house.

How can students create a beanstalk? Considering the fact that the characters need to be at both ends of the beanstalk and that it would be best if they kept their feet on the ground for safety reasons, why not design a bean vine that runs along the floor? Picture a nice, long roll of white butcher's paper with a vine painted along it. A leaf stamp would make it a quick job. Another possibility is to cut out large leaves from green felt and lay them out on the floor down the center aisle of the audience. This vine must be rolled down between scenes to create a nice surprise. Another possibility is to run a short vine in front and up onto the stage.

What about Jack's cow? A large cardboard box, some roller skates, and paint can be turned into a two-dimensional cow-on-wheels that Jack can pull onstage by a rope. The giant's set can be created simply as well. Arrange a few pieces of firewood like a campfire, and find the biggest rocking chair in the school to borrow for the giant.

The period of the story determines what costumes are used. The students must work with borrowed clothing, so draw up lists and send them home to ask for donations. Anything not used in the play can be returned or donated to Goodwill. The following script for *Jack and the Beanstalk* is based on an adaptation done by a fifth-grade class in Colorado. Simple sets and costumes are suggested, but of course, one good volunteer with a sewing machine would go a long way.

JACK AND THE BEANSTALK

Summary

This is a six-act play with five characters based on the story about the famous boy named Jack who acquired some magic beans, met a giant and his wife, and acquired a golden goose.

Set

Jack's front porch is shown by a bench with several potted flowers. A giant's castle is implied with a few pieces of fire wood with a large black cook pot in the center. Dry ice inside the pot will release steam. A green vine (painted on paper, or glued together in green felt) will be rolled off the stage and across the front. Action takes place on and in front of the stage.

Props

The following must be assembled: six dried beans, a thick rope, cardboard cut and painted as a cow (on wheels), large cook pot set on firewood, dry ice, stirring spoon, coins for the giant's pocket, a sack with a $ sign painted on it (for the giant's pillow), a wooden bowl, a whipped cream-filled pie pan, a plush animal goose, and a golden egg.

Costumes

Jack wears modern play clothes. George, the giant, wears long pants to hide his stilts, made from two large coffee cans strapped into boots. Strap these to the actor's own shoes for stomping. Jack's mom wears overalls because she's a poor farmer. Martha wears a chef's hat and apron. The merchant wears flashy colors.

Characters

Jack
Jack's mom
Merchant
George Giant *(on stilts)*
Martha *(regular sized person)*

JACK AND THE BEANSTALK

Scene 1—Jack's Farm House

(Enter Jack and his mom. They sit on a bench near flower pots. Jack's mom sips from a mug. Jack has a bowl of cereal.)

Mom: Jack, we need to sell the cow.

Jack: But Mom, she's all we have left. She's still giving us milk and she doesn't eat much. We have to keep her.

Mom: Her milk is what will fetch us a good price. Once winter hits, there will be no more grass and we cannot afford hay. She'll starve. We must sell her now.

Jack: Okay, Mom. I'll take her to town.

Mom: Thank you, son. Remember what your father taught you about negotiations. If you go now, you'll arrive with the crowds and get a better price. *(Lights down.)*

Scene 2—To Market

(Jack enters, pulling cow. Merchant follows.)

Merchant: That's a mighty fine cow you have there, young man. I'm in the market for a cow such as that. Will you sell her to me?

Jack: I'm on my way into town to do just that, sir.

Merchant: Why don't I save you the walk? I'll buy her right here, right now.

Jack: You have no wallet. How will you buy her?

Merchant: *(Pulls beans out of pocket.)* I'll give you these magic beans. They'll bring you more treasures than money could ever buy.

Jack: That's ridiculous. Move out of my way, Mister. I promised my mother I'd sell our cow in town, and that's what I'm going to do.

Merchant: How can magic be ridiculous? These aren't ordinary beans. You're a boy with a good imagination. That's obvious. These three beans can make your dreams come true. That's a good exchange for your cow.

Jack: Any dreams?

Merchant: Any.

Jack: Like piles of cash, all the hamburgers I can eat, and adventure?

Merchant: If those are your dreams, then that's what you'll achieve.

Jack: Now I know you're crazy. Excuse me, sir, and . . . good-bye!

Merchant: That's what my last customer thought at first, too. Now he is the King of Arbania.

Jack: Sure he is, and I'm the Queen of Sheba.

Merchant: Ah, you are a skeptic. You will grow up to be a great man some day, if your caution doesn't scare you away from opportunities.

Jack: Three beans don't sound like opportunity to me.

Merchant: Very well, perhaps your neighbor will want this treasure.

Jack: My neighbor might, but he has nothing to trade. Listen, it's hot out here, and I'm tired of walking. I'll let you save me some trouble after all. Give me six beans, take the cow, and leave or it's no deal.

Merchant: You drive a hard bargain, young man. Six beans may bring you more grief than luck, but if that's what you want . . .

Jack: It's six beans or nothing. I'm not afraid of any grief. How can more riches be bad?

Merchant: As you wish. *(Hands over beans. Exits with cow.)*

Jack: *(Returns to bench.)* Mom! I sold Bessie!

Mom: *(Enters.)* How can you be back so soon? What did you do, just let her go on the road? Where's the cow, Jack?

Jack: She's with her new owner, because I sold her, just like you told me to.

Mom: That would be a first! How much did you get?

Jack: I got something better than money, Mom. I got six magic beans. Look! See?

Mom: *(Takes beans.)* You traded our cow for six lousy beans? Jack, are you crazy? Six kidney beans won't even flavor our soup, and if you weren't such an idiot, you would have known that. This is what I think of your stupid beans! *(Throws beans offstage.)*

Jack: No, wait! Mom, the man said . . .

Mom: Jack, that's enough. There is no dinner, no cow, and winter is nearly here. I'm too tired to listen to all your excuses tonight. Go to bed so I can think.

Jack: But, Mom. I . . .

Mom: Not now. I have to think.

Jack: I'm sorry, I didn't mean to . . .

Mom: Yeah, I know. You didn't mean to give our cow away for nothing, but you did and now we'll go hungry. Go on. I'll think of something. *(Jack exits. Lights down.)*

Scene 3—The Giant

(Lights up on the beanstalk. Stage is dark, but Martha is there, stirring a pot full of dry ice, set on some firewood.)

Mom: *(Enters in front of stage.)* Jack, come look! There's a huge vine covering our entire field.

Jack: *(Offstage.)* Sure, Mom, a huge vine grew over night. *(Enters.)* Hey, what do you know? You're right. Look at the size of it! I wonder how far it goes. I'll be right back, Mom. *(Mom slowly backs offstage, as Jack follows vine to other end of stage.)* This thing goes on forever. I just have to get past this cloud . . . *(Peers onstage.)* and . . . *(Lights up on Martha stirring her steaming pot. To audience.)* I don't think I'm in Kansas anymore. Wonder what's in that cooking pot—it sure smells good. *(Heavy footsteps offstage.)* That sounds like an elephant. I'll just hide over here. *(Hides below edge of stage. Enter giant.)*

George: Fee, Fie, Foe, Fum. I smell the breath of an Englishman. No, wait, it's . . . an unwashed Kansas farm boy. Oh goody. Those are my favorite. Martha? Is that Kansas farm boy I smell cooking in your pot? *(Sniffs pot and jingles coins in pocket.)*

Jack: *(To audience.)* He smelled me? But this isn't my week for a bath. Why I oughtta . . . Wait a minute; did I hear money in his pocket? I'll show him unwashed—unwashed and rich. I'll just wait until he falls asleep, then it's all mine.

George: Martha, what you got in that there cookin' pot of yours? It sure smells good. My little snookums is such a good cook. *(Kisses top of her head.)*

Martha: My, aren't you the charmer, George! You'd better get that nose of yours checked though. I haven't seen any farm boys around here for ages. This pot's full of my usual—it's egg drop soup!

George: Well that's strange. Say, you ain't dropping my golden eggs again, are you?

Martha: No dear, these were the other hen's.

George: Did you make me a toenail pie to go with it? Huh, did ya? Huh?

Martha: Certainly, Georgie. I know that's your other favorite! Now here's your soup. Eat that up first; then you can have pie.

George: *(Pretends to scoop soup with bowl and then drink it.)* Mmmm, that was good. Now where's my pie?

Martha: It's cooling in the breeze right over there. Help yourself.

George: *(Picks up pie and scoops it into mouth with hands, burps.)* Ahhh! Now that's good cookin'. You outdone yourself, Martha. I'm gonna rest my eyes a time and let my supper settle before I go check on that smell. *(Stretches out on floor, rests head on sack of money, snores.)*

Jack: *(Aside.)* Toenail pie? Golden eggs and a sack of money for a pillow? This guy's crazy. He won't miss a couple of those coins. Now where did his wife go? *(Climbs onto stage, freezes.)*

Martha: You'd better keep your distance, boy. You wouldn't be the first one he caught, nor the last. I wouldn't recommend sticking around long enough to go for that money, either. It's his favorite pillow, even though it's lumpy and hard. He says it gives him sweet dreams.

Jack: Oh, excuse me, ma'am. Hey! You're my size. How come a normal-sized lady like you is married to a giant like him?

Martha: Now don't you be bad-mouthing my husband, boy. He's the sweetest man I ever met.

Jack: Well, now I'm sure you're right, ma'am. He does look gentle enough. I'm just a poor starving boy trying to feed myself and my dear, widowed mother. We would be grateful if you could help us out. Can I do a chore for a few coins?

Martha: A chore, huh? Let's see, I've fed the chickens, gone to market, made the soup, and scrubbed the . . . no I haven't. All I have left to do is the dishes. I suppose I could give you a coin for doing that.

Jack: Can I fetch anything for you, carry heavy loads, hoe your garden?

Martha: It's a couple of days early for hoeing, but since you're here . . .

Jack: Just a few coins will feed my Mom and me for weeks. I promise I won't ever bother you again, unless you want me to. Scout's honor, and cross my heart.

Martha: Well . . . as long as you're a scout! I can spare a couple of coins. I have some in my pocket from the market. Now you go find the hoe, it's leaning against the shed out back.

Jack: Oh, thank you. I'll hoe your garden and be back in a jiffy.

Martha: Wait, hold on a minute. If you come back in here and wake my husband, he won't take kindly to that. I'm going to trust you, you being a scout and all. Here, take your payment in advance then get to work. *(Hands him coins.)*

Jack: *(Bows.)* Thank you, ma'am. I'm as good as my word, just you watch. 'Bye. *(Exits. Lights dim as more mist flows across stage. Lights up on Jack sitting at top of vine. To audience.)* Now that was one profitable day. What will I tell Mom, though? If I tell her about the giant, she'll think I'm crazy. It'll just have to be my secret. How do I explain the coins then? I know, I'll tell her I found that merchant again and made him pay me for the cow this time. Yeah, that's it. I made him pay, right. Hey, Mom. Guess what. *(Exits. Lights dim.)*

Scene 4—Top of the Vine

(Lights up. Jack is back on the edge of the stage.)

Jack: Oh sure! I know what you're thinking. I promised Mrs. Giant I wouldn't come back. What? You never promised with your fingers crossed before? I believe you; see? *(Shows crossed fingers.)* You know, I got to thinking about that golden goose and didn't get a lick of sleep. Mom and I sure could use a goose like that, so I'm back for another quick look around. I'll be in and out in no time. *(Peers over edge of stage and freezes.)*

George: *(Stomps onstage.)* Fee, fie, foe, fum! I smell something nasty again. Why, I'll just follow my nose and find it. Oh drat! It's that farm boy looking for my golden goose. He'd better keep his sticky fingers off my beautiful bird! Where are you boy? You can't hide from me. *(Exits.)*

Jack: *(To audience.)* Sticky fingers? How'd he know? Someone spilled the beans. Well, as long as I have a reputation, I might as well . . . *(Sneaks onto stage, then exits. Sounds of chickens and a goose squawking. Runs back in with goose under arm.)* Hah! That was easy. I'm outta here! Shhhh! *(Slinks along vine.)*

George: *(Stomps back onstage.)* Stop, thief! I'll catch you, if it's the last thing I do. *(Leaps offstage and chases Jack through audience. Both exit.)*

Jack: *(Enters at end of vine.)* He'll never find me. Phew, I made it. Now what will I do with this vine? Look out, goose. *(Tosses goose to the side.)* Cut it down? With what? The hoe? Ahhh, watch this . . . *(Rolls vine.)*

George: *(Stomps onstage and peers at Jack.)* I ate your uncle; he was yummy, now I want **YOU** in my tummy!

Jack: I don't think so. You have to catch me first. *(Rolls faster. George climbs off stage, rolls onto ground where vine is gone, then sprawls at Jack's feet. Enter Jack's mom.)*

Mom: What was that, Jack? Oh my gosh! That's the biggest man I've ever seen. Why is he on the ground? What did you do?

Jack: That's no big man, Mom. That's a giant. He's been eating Kansas farm boys for ages. Well, not any more because your son Jack just destroyed his magic vine. He won't ever bother anyone again. I think he's dead from the fall, but I wouldn't get too close, just in case.

Mom: A giant and his magic vine? What are you talking about? Quit giving me stories and tell me the truth. Besides, it wasn't his vine; it was yours. Why would this big man chase you?

Jack: This isn't fair. I just saved you from being his next snack and all you can do is accuse me of things?

Mom: A boy like you has no business talking about fair, Jack. I'm not accusing you. I'm asking you to explain what happened. Hey, what's that? There's something shiny underneath that little goose. Where'd she come from? . . . Jack?

Jack: Looks like a golden egg, Mom. So, that's why he was so protective of his goose. Her eggs are gold, not her color. Mom, we're rich!

Mom: Well, well, Jacky boy. That goose will just about make up for the cow you gave away, but you're still grounded until spring thaw. *(Grabs Jack's ear and leads him offstage.)*

Jack: Ow, ow, ow! You can't ground me. I just saved this whole town from a huge and terrible giant. I ought to get a reward.

Mom: You have a point there, boy. Okay, for tonight only, you get raisins in your oatmeal. Don't expect any such privileges again until you've gotten rid of your sticky fingers and foolish schemes. *(Both exit.)*

Giant: *(Sits up in spotlight.)* The moral of the story is: Sticky fingers could get you grounded, so wash your hands before you eat. *(Falls back, then sits back up.)* Also, crime doesn't pay . . . or does it? *(Down, up.)* . . . and watch where you toss your beans. *(Down, lights down too.)*

Story Adaptation

Let's try that again with the story of "Hansel and Gretel." Theirs is a story of hope in the face of terrible odds. The children have desperate parents who abandon them. They get lost in the woods, meet a cannibal witch, and survive by their wits and by working together. Consider handing out copies of the worksheet at the end of this chapter so that students can fill it out as you review the Playwriting section with them. When they are finished, each student will be able to write their own version of this play.

Playwriting

Ask students to write a short paragraph on the theme of the story. They may come up with something entirely different from what is suggested above.

The next decision is the time period they want for their version, remembering the ground rules. Hansel and Gretel meet a witch, something that doesn't come up nowadays except at Halloween. Perhaps it can be set in the time of the Salem witch trials.

Once the time period is known, the stage sets can be considered. First, take a tour of your school's theater or auditorium. Make a list of all the things you will have at your disposal for staging, such as the availability of a curtain, lights, and sound equipment. Have students keep this in mind as they write the action of their plays.

Now read the story and list the locations that are described. There's the family's cottage, a forest clearing for their picnic, and then the witch's gingerbread house. This last set will be created using large cardboard boxes and a few pieces of furniture borrowed from classrooms or perhaps a teacher's lounge such as the woodcutter's table and chairs. Paint a large refrigerator carton to look like a gingerbread house, and set a few loose pieces of candy on the top to be eaten. This will be lightweight enough to push on stage before Scene 3.

A cage is made from a smaller box with a window cut out of the side. The flaps of the box become the gate, and it is painted also. Rather than adding another box for the oven, characters can go behind the house box when "working" in the oven.

The period of the story determines what costumes are used. The students must work with borrowed clothing, so draw up lists and send them home to ask for donations. Anything not used in the play can be returned or donated to Goodwill.

Keep track of the props needed as the script is written. For instance, the following items must be collected for breakfast and a picnic: a saucepan for porridge, mugs and a coffee pot, a blanket, water jug, picnic basket, and a bundle of sticks for kindling. Don't forget the witch's brooms and a rag that will go in her pocket.

As you read the dialog in the following script, see if you can get a feel for the character's personalities. Ask the class to listen as the script is read as well and then have them describe the characters. The dialog is the only way to illustrate what a character is like in a play. Students should then be prepared to write their own versions.

HANSEL AND GRETEL

Summary

This is the classic tale about a brother and sister who are lost and hungry in the woods until they find a gingerbread house to eat. The house is occupied and more trouble follows, but the children stick together and escape to live happily ever after.

Set

The cottage is created with a table and chairs. Several potted plants with a picnic blanket spread on the floor create the woods in Scene 2. The gingerbread house is made by painting an empty refrigerator box. Several pieces of candy must be laid on top to be eaten. A smaller box is painted to look like a cage, with a window cut out of the side and the flaps used as the cage doors.

Props

In Scene 1, a saucepan, wooden spoon, coffee pot, and mug are on the table. Several feet away are a bunch of sticks tied together for kindling, a blanket, water jug, and picnic basket with towel. Hansel enters with a rag doll. In Scene 3, lean two brooms and a stick near the gingerbread house. The witch tucks a rag for dusting and a key ring into pockets.

Costumes

Gretel wears a long skirt and braids. Her stepmother and the witch need long skirts, and the witch must have pockets in an apron. Father wears long pants, and Hansel wears shorts.

Characters

Stepmother
Father
Gretel
Hansel
Witch

HANSEL AND GRETEL

Scene 1—Breakfast

(In a log cabin in the woods Father sits at a kitchen table, the stepmother stirs a pot on the stove as they talk. It is morning.)

Stepmother: These rotten kids are eating all the food in the house. I wish they would just get lost. *(Calls out.)* Children, come to breakfast!

Father: Are you sure we have to take the children to the woods this morning? There must be another way!

Stepmother: We just don't have enough food for us all. I thought we settled this last night. Besides, they're making me crazy with all their running around. Did you know that Hansel put a frog under my pillow last night? And I think I'll scream if I have to listen to Gretel's whining for even one more day. *(Enter children—running and shouting.)*

Gretel: Give that back, Hansel! It's mine!

Hansel: *(Runs around table, away from Gretel.)* Come and get it if you can. All you have to do is catch me, silly!

Gretel: *(Whines.)* Papa! Hansel won't give me back my doll! Make him give it back! Please?

Father: Now, now, children slow down. You are in the house. You know you are not supposed to run in the house. Hansel stop teasing your sister. Come along you two, it's time for breakfast.

Hansel: *(Tosses Gretel's rag doll to her.)* Here you are, Gretel. Next time see if you can catch me.

Gretel: I can catch you in my sleep!

Stepmother: There won't be any next time because there won't be any more running in the house, right children?

Hansel and Gretel: Yes, stepmother. *(Hansel moves to sit and bumps his father's arm, spilling coffee on his father's shirt.)*

Stepmother: Hansel! Look what you've done. I just finished washing and ironing that shirt. Now I have to start all over again. As if I didn't already have enough to do trying to keep us all fed. Sit down, eat your breakfast, and watch where you're going.

Father: Oh Martha, stop fussing. The boy didn't do it on purpose. By the way, from what I tasted, you made great coffee this morning! Children, your mother and I have been discussing whether we should go for a picnic. It's a perfect day to spend outside. We can gather wood and berries as we go. I'll bring along the duck I shot yesterday, and we can roast it over a fire in our favorite clearing. What do you think?

Hansel: Ya, Papa, and I'll carry the water jug and the kindling.

Gretel: *(Whispers to Hansel.)* But, Hansel, the forest is so dark. It frightens me.

Hansel: *(Whispers.)* It will be all right. I saved my bread crust from last night's supper. I'll drop pieces as we walk. We can follow the breadcrumb trail to find our way if we get lost.

Gretel: All right. I'll carry the blanket.

Stepmother: Well, I should think so! I'm certainly not carrying everything. Come along children! Quit dawdling! We don't have all day, you know.

Father: Martha, relax! Let's try to have a pleasant time. We're in no hurry.

Gretel: This blanket is so much heavier than I remembered. I don't know if I can carry it!

Hansel: Here, Gretel. You carry the water jug and I'll take the blanket. *(Whispers.)* It will cover my hands as I drop the crumbs. *(The family gathers their supplies and exits. Lights dim.)*

Scene 2—Picnic

(Lights up on the family as they finish a picnic in a clearing in the woods.)

Hansel: Thank you, Stepmother. That was delicious. Are you as sleepy as I am, Gretel?

Gretel: Oh, yes, I am sleepy and full.

Father: Why don't you two lie down for a rest while your mother and I clean up?

Stepmother: Wait a minute . . . why do I always have to . . .

Father: Martha! Don't worry; I'll help, remember? *(He looks at her meaningfully.)*

Gretel: *(Not noticing the look between her parents, she stretches out on the blanket.)* Oh, thank you, Papa. I love to listen to the birds as I fall asleep. It smells so good here, too. It must be the fresh grass growing in the sunlight. It is a little cold though.

Hansel: Come closer, Gretel. We can share my jacket. We can keep each other warm.

Father: *(Whispers to Stepmother.)* Don't they look like angels the way they're all curled up together like that?

Stepmother: *(Whispers.)* Now, don't you go getting all soft on me. We talked enough about this, we made a decision, and I don't want to discuss it any more.

Father: I know, I know, you're right. We have no choice. Let's just sit with them a few more minutes.

Stepmother: No, now's our chance to slip away. Let's get out of here before they wake up.

Father: I'm not sure this is the best idea. It's so cruel. Gretel will be very frightened. I don't think I can do this.

Stepmother: Remember this morning's coffee! Why can't you just make up your mind and stick to it. You always question our decisions. We have to stick together.

Father: Fine, fine. Let's just go. I can't bear to look at them any longer. *(Lights go down as they exit.)*

Scene 3—All Alone

(Lights come back up—it is morning.)

Gretel: *(Sits up and yawns.)* Hansel, where are we? Where are Mama and Papa? What time is it?

Hansel: *(Rubs eyes.)* What? What's the matter?

Gretel: We're in the woods all by ourselves. Father and Stepmother are gone. *(Cries.)*

Hansel: Don't worry, remember our emergency plan? We just have to follow our breadcrumbs home and we'll be all right. Please, stop crying.

Gretel: *(Wipes eyes and stands.)* I'm not crying, I just got something in my eye, that's all!

Hansel: Sure you did, sis. Let's see now, if it's morning and the shadows go that way, then we get home by going . . .

Gretel: It all looks different now.

Hansel: It's not a problem. We just have to find the bread crumbs. *(Searches the ground.)*

Gretel: *(Searches.)* Did you run out before we got here? I don't see any.

Hansel: Keep looking. What do you think happened to Father and Stepmother?

Gretel: I don't know, but I don't like it. Let's find those breadcrumbs.

Hansel: I don't see a single crumb. Do you think a squirrel ate them?

Gretel: Hans—we are so stupid! If we've been here all night, then the squirrels and birds had plenty of time to find our bread and eat it all gone!

Hansel: Stupid is not the word for it. Well . . . I hadn't planned on spending the night; it might have worked if we'd only been here a little while.

Gretel: You're right, but now what do we do?

Hansel: Can you remember where the sun was when we came here? Was it in front of us, back of us, to one side?

Gretel: I don't remember.

Hansel: Me neither. It must have been cloudy. Let's look for footprints, then.

Gretel: Okay, but let's stick together. I don't want to get separated from you, too!

Hansel: Fine with me. Let's try that trail, okay?

Fairy Tale Plays

Gretel: Looks as good as any. At least we have our blanket and water. *(Picks up the water jug.)*

Hansel: *(Folds the blanket and drapes it around neck.)* That's right. It could be worse . . .

(Both exit, studying the ground. Lights down.)

Scene 4—A Gingerbread House

(Hansel and Gretel enter, still studying the ground. A gingerbread house is dimly lit on the opposite side of the stage.)

Gretel: *(Looks up and notices house.)* What's that, Hansel? It looks like a house.

Hansel: Let's go see if anyone's home. Maybe they can tell us where we are and will give us something to eat.

Gretel: What a strange looking house it is. It reminds me of the houses Mom used to make at Christmas out of gingerbread and candy . . . and it smells so good. Do you see any peppermint growing around here?

Hansel: I don't know what peppermint looks like, but doesn't this icicle look like frosting? I'm so hungry, I have to try it. *(Breaks it off and tastes it.)* Yum. It *is* frosting! Gretel, I think this house is made out of candy. *(Enter Witch.)*

Witch: Who's that nibblin' on my house? *(Aside.)* Oooh! Children! Nice, plump, juicy looking children! *(Out loud.)* What beautiful children you are! You must be hungry to eat a complete stranger's house. Well, be my guests, children. I can always make more!

Gretel: We're sorry. We didn't know anyone lived here. We *are* hungry though. Did you make this yourself?

Witch: Yes, I made it myself, and how would you know if anyone lived here? I didn't hear you knock at my door.

Hansel: Please excuse our terrible manners, Ma'am. We weren't thinking. We haven't eaten since yesterday morning when we went on a picnic with our parents. They've disappeared, and we cannot find our way home. Do you know where the woodcutter's house is?

Witch: Woodcutter, eh? Certainly I know him! He's married to my sister, isn't he?

Gretel: You're our stepmother's sister? We never knew she had one!

Witch: That figures. We never did get along very well. Sister rivalry, you know. Well, now, why don't you two just go ahead and fill yourselves up on your Auntie's delicious house. *(Squeezes Gretel's arm.)* You need more meat on your bones if you want to grow to be big and strong like your father.

Hansel: Thank you, Ma'am.

Gretel: You are so kind. *(Eats. Witch cackles with delight, rubbing hands.)*

Witch: When you are full, perhaps you wouldn't mind helping an old lady with some chores? It's getting harder and harder for me to take care of things around here.

Hansel: We'd be happy to help.

Witch: Then perhaps you, my dear little girl, will help me sweep inside the house. You, young man, can help me clean out this old cage. I used to keep a pet bear in there, but he got too big and I had to release him. If you would just climb in there and sweep the cage floor, I might be able to sell the cage and buy some food for myself.

Hansel: Where's your broom? I'll start right away. *(Looks around for broom.)* Oh, here it is. *(Sweeps and walks into cage.)*

Witch: *(Horrified.)* No! Not that one, that's my mag—I mean my fly—I mean the old one. I have a nice new one right here. *(Reaches inside house and pulls out a broom.)* Now give me that one. *(They switch brooms.)* That's right, go ahead and try it. That one will work much better. Don't know why I keep this old thing, but I do hate to throw anything away.

Gretel: *(Wipes mouth.)* Do you have another broom for inside the house? I'm ready to help now too.

Witch: No, Deary. *(Reaches into pocket and pulls out rag.)* Why don't you use this old rag and take care of the dusting instead.

Gretel: Certainly. That's the job I do at home all the time. My father says I am the best duster in the whole forest! *(Skips offstage.)*

Witch: That's fine, dear. *(Waits until she's inside, then rushes over and closes the cage on Hansel very quietly. Cackles.)* There now! That ought to hold you until you are nice and plump. The girl is much too skinny. I'll just keep her around to help with the chores. My eyes are so bad I can hardly see to stir my pot! *(Sneaks away, lights dim.)*

Scene 5—A Plan

(Lights up. Hansel looks through the cage window, while Gretel holds his hand through the opening.)

Hansel: Don't worry, Gretel. I thought of something last night. Hand me that stick over there. Next time she tells me to give her my hand, I'll hold out the stick. That'll fool her for a while!

Gretel: Oh Hansel! It had better work! She's so old and crooked that she can hardly walk. I'm not worried about me, because I can run away from her, but you can't. I can't get the key to this cage because she keeps it in her pocket, and since there's nothing wrong with her hearing, I can't sneak up on her.

Hansel: I know. I've watched you try. You be careful. Keep pretending you are frightened of her and keep your distance. Otherwise, do everything she asks. I'm sure we'll be all right. I can feel it. Maybe Papa is looking for us right now and will rescue us any time.

Gretel: I hope so. We can't be very far from home, and Papa knows every path in the woods. He'll find us. *(Enter Witch.)*

Witch: What are you children whispering about? Trying to get away, eh? This old witch may be nearly blind, but my ears are better than ever. Even if you could run away, little girl, I'd sniff you out, and I'd hear you, too. So forget about it. I smell dusty curtains. Take them down, girl, and give them a good rinsing in the stream.

Gretel: *(Whimpers, but winks at Hansel.)* Yes, ma'am. Right away, ma'am. Please don't hurt me! *(Squeals as the witch grabs her and pinches, then exits.)*

Witch: *(Aside.)* Hmmm! Even if that boy never fattens up, the girl would be tasty. I think I'll start up the oven right now. She can be the appetizer. I'll save the boy for supper! *(Cackles and rubs hands.)* Girl! Come here! Get me firewood for the oven. I have some baking to do!

Gretel: *(Enters with kindling bundle.)* Yes, ma'am. Here I come.

Witch: Now stack the wood in the bottom there. *(Gretel goes behind gingerbread house.)* That's it. Don't pack it too tight or it won't get enough air to burn! Let me see, girl. Get out of my way! *(Peers behind house.)* Perfect. You must have done this before. Now find the flint and light it up.

Gretel: But I don't know how to use a flint. That's always been Hansel's job. Maybe you could let him out for just a minute to help us. I'll just take the keys. *(Reaches for them.)*

Witch: *(Grabs the keys and spins around.)* Oh no you don't, girlie! Nice try. Is that what you two were cooking up before? *(Cackles.)* Heh, heh, cooking up . . . ha! You'll have to do better than that. I may be blind, but I wasn't born yesterday.

Hansel: *(Mumbles.)* You can say that again!

Witch: *(Angry.)* What? You dare to insult me? You were stupid enough to climb into that cage all by yourself? Hah, I'll show you. Light that fire, girl, and stop your whimpering. If there's anything I can't stand, it's whimpering girls. You'd better help me or I might decide to cook you first.

Gretel: No, please let me go into the woods and snare a nice tasty rabbit for you instead. It'll taste much better than we will.

Witch: I don't think so, little lady. I much prefer the taste of roast boy. Now stop fidgeting and light that oven! *(Gretel scratches two rocks together behind the house.)* Now stop that, girl! I heard that. Strike the flint, not the oven! *(Gretel cries out, and appears, sucking on her thumb.)* Oh for crying out loud. Heh, heh, crying out loud, get it, eh? Get out of my way, child. You are beginning to really irritate me! Give me that flint! *(Gretel hands it to her and steps back.)*

Witch: Here! Just strike it like this, right over the wood. That's all you have to do. See? *(Strikes rocks together.)*

Gretel: But you are too far from the wood to catch any sparks, ma'am. Are you sure that's right?

Witch: Certainly I'm right. Haven't I been lighting this oven for over a hundred years by now? Don't you think I know how to light my own oven? What a stupid girl! I'll just do it myself! I'll just reach in a little further, like this. *(Strikes rocks again, then steps back* *from behind house.)* There now, see? I can smell the smoke. It's lit. Now back to your washing, girl! *(Exits.)*

Gretel: Yes, ma'am. *(Gretel rushes to Hansel, they whisper and gesture, then nod as witch enters.)*

Witch: That fire should be ready by now, girl. Go see if it is hot enough to bake.

Gretel: Yes ma'am. *(Looks behind house then returns.)* Oh, I don't know. It doesn't seem to be very hot at all. My stepmother always bakes at a much higher temperature.

Witch: Well, my sister is just as stupid as you are, girl. Roasting is done at a nice low temperature. Everyone knows that! Get out of my way. Let me check it myself. *(She pushes Gretel back; Gretel slips the witch's key out of her pocket as she brushes past. Then, as the Witch leans in, Gretel steps back further.)* Yes, yes. This is just right! *(Gretel runs up behind her and pushes her all the way behind the house. A door slams offstage.)* Oh, wicked, wicked girl! Help me, I'm melting. Help me, help me . . . *(Her voice fades into a wail.)*

Gretel: *(Whimpers, then rushes to the cage and releases Hansel.)*

Hansel: Gretel! I can't believe you did that! It was brilliant! *(He climbs out of his cage and then stands uneasily.)*

Gretel: No, it wasn't brilliant. It was horrible. I can't believe I did it either. That poor old woman!

Hansel: Poor old woman? She's a witch, Gretel. She was planning to eat both of us for dinner tonight. She was an evil old woman, and she got what she deserved. Don't cry for her.

Gretel: Oh, Hansel. I miss Mama and Papa.

Hansel: Me too, sis, but with a brave sister like you, I'm not worried. We'll do just fine. What do you say we try to snare a rabbit for our own supper, just like you offered that old witch? Do you really know how?

Gretel: Sure I do! I watched Papa do it a thousand times. Let's . . . *(Whistle sounds offstage.)* What was that? Did you just hear a whistle?

Hansel: No, all I can hear is that wretched witch.

Gretel: Hush! Come over here and listen!

Hansel: There! I heard something. Maybe it's Papa! Let's whistle back. *(Hansel whistles. They listen for an answer and hear one.)*

Father: *(Offstage.)* Hansel, Gretel, is that you? Whistle again so I can find you!

(They both whistle as he walks onstage and the children run to embrace him.)

Hansel: Papa! You found us! What happened? Why did you leave us?

Gretel: Yes, Papa, why?

Father: I didn't want to. It was your stepmother's idea. As soon as we returned to the house, she started to act very strangely. Thank God you weren't there. Oh, children, I was so worried about you. Come over here and sit with me. Let me get a good look at you.

Gretel: We're fine, Papa. What do you mean she acted strangely?

Father: She aged before my very eyes and turned into a grizzly old hag! She started to mumble a spell at me—something about getting a new familiar, a cat—and she pointed her gnarled finger at me. I saw a wisp of smoke curl off her finger and knew she was a witch. I acted fast and swung my ax just in time. She disappeared in a puff of smoke, and I've been looking for you ever since. What's that smell?

Hansel: Papa, you should have seen it. We met Stepmother's sister, another witch, and she wanted to eat us. Gretel pushed her into her own oven. That's what you smell.

Father: Gretel did that? What a brave little girl. I guess we won't have to worry about witches any more. Come on children, let's go home. The woods will be much safer from now on. What a story. No one will ever believe us. *(Exit, arms around each other. Lights dim, curtain down.)*

Form 3.1

Script Planning Sheet

1. What fairy tale will you adapt?

2. Write a short paragraph that explains the theme of your story.

3. List the characters' names.

4. What is the time period?

5. List the places in the story.

May be copied for classroom use. Literary Ideas and Scripts for Young Playwrights by Lisa Kaniut Cobb (Portsmouth, NH: Teacher Ideas Press) © 2004.

Form 3.1 *Continued*

6. Decide how you will design the stage.

7. What costumes are needed?

8. List the props needed.

9. What jobs can stage hands do?

10. Are stage lights available? Decide what will cue the lights.

4

Fairy Tale Variations for Readers Theatre

Story Adaptation

Why would anyone want to change fairy tales? Is there something wrong with them? Absolutely not! In fact there are so many things right with them that they make great spring boards for new story and play ideas.

Have students analyze their favorite fairy tale by outlining the main events, theme, characters, setting, and time, as they did in Chapter 3. They may want to use the worksheet. Next, they must decide which aspects to change. Suggest that students consider changing the beginning, middle, or end, the main character, the location, or the time. What if the bad guy, known as the antagonist, told the story from his perspective? Would he still be the bad guy? What if a minor character became a major one? How would that change things?

List the possibilities and vote on them if the story is a class project. Then discuss how the rest of the story is affected. There are endless variations, so even if small groups work on the same story, the results will be unique. The trick is to make the new story unpredictable. A surprise ending is always a great reward for the reader or audience, and it makes the writing fun, too.

If you decide to ask students to create their own story and play, plan class time for readings by the playwrights. Another option is to work in teams to not only develop an original story, but also to exercise students' interpersonal skills as they negotiate changes, solve problems, write, edit, and check spelling for each other. When large classes are broken into teams, their plays can be performed for other teams, for other classes, or even for school performances in front of parents. When students see their work rehearsed, they observe strengths and weaknesses and they can then make improvements. For instance, they may notice that a section of the new story moves too slowly, or the dialog is stilted. Many younger students are reluctant to make changes to their stories, but these exercises help them become comfortable with constructive criticism, a skill that is invaluable throughout school and adult life. Critique guidelines are included at the end of Chapter 11.

Consider the story "The Three Billy Goats Gruff" as a simple model. What if the billy goats are turned into snapping turtles? The plot can remain the same, but the setting has to change because turtles could not care less about finding fresh green grass across a bridge on the other side of a river. In order to fit the action to the new characters, a series of questions will help create a completely new scenario.

If the turtles don't live in a grassy field, where do they live? Turtles live in small lakes and ponds. What would make turtles leave the safety of their pond? Maybe their pond dried up. Perhaps the turtles live in a forest pond that dried up because beavers dammed the river that fed it. The river would create new ponds somewhere else and the turtles would have to cross the river to find them. The river has to be dangerous, just like the bridge is dangerous to the goats, which is the important conflict in the original story. The river could flow too fast for the turtles to be able to swim across, or the troll from the original story could become an alligator that likes to eat turtles. He might live under a fallen tree for shade. The tree creates a natural bridge for the turtles to cross. Notice how the original story helps make the decisions for the new characters.

For this example, the personalities of the turtles can remain the same. There are three of them, the youngest is small and timid, the middle one is larger but still not very meaty, and the oldest turtle is large and strong. They each have to convince the alligator to wait for the larger turtle that follows.

Don't forget that a surprise ending is best. How do the turtles discover that the alligator is there? What if the turtles watch as a crow perches on the fallen log and the alligator leaps into the air to eat him? The crow flies away, but the alligator's hiding place is revealed. Since the turtles cannot simply fly away, they have to find another solution. Suspense builds. The solution has to be consistent with what a turtle would really do, such as moving slowly. Perhaps these turtles could be as smart as the famous tortoise that raced the hare and won through persistence. If they are snapping turtles, perhaps they are feisty and can work together to fight off the alligator. This is a new twist to the story ending. Speaking of endings, can these turtles live happily ever after in the alligator's backyard? That seems improbable.

Playwriting

At this point, several decisions must be made before a script is begun. The turtle story is probably more suited to a young audience because it is a simple, short story, and it has animals as the main characters. A readers theatre script for third graders would allow the use of a narrator. Begin with a list of the characters, plus a narrator who can help move the story along. Perhaps the characters should have names that reflect their personalities. Names also make dialog between the characters easier. Rather than calling each other big brother, or, say, Mr. Alligator, characters call each other by name.

The next questions are where and when to begin the story. If the oldest turtle goes off to search for a new pond—a logical assumption—the narrator can set that up in a sentence and introduce the other two turtles. The turtles can discuss their difficulties—the dried-up pond, beaver dams, hunger. These are all things that motivate the characters to act, while revealing who they are, where they live, and what they want—the story's conflict. The second scene will follow the oldest turtle as he meets the crow and alligator and then formulates a plan. The third scene will bring all the characters back together at the river and show how the problem is solved.

Let's consider the set. The use of stools allows actors to sit and read their character's lines, rather than their being expected to act. The only decision left is how to arrange the readers on the stage. An interesting dynamic might arise if the narrator and Mrs. Crow sit off to one side, while the turtles and alligator are arranged as they were for *The Last Toll,* with the alligator on the floor in front of the three stools for the turtles. No costumes or props are required. Read *The Three Snapping Turtles* to see one way the story could end.

THE THREE SNAPPING TURTLES

Summary

Three snapping turtles must find a new pond because theirs has dried up. How will they cross the river and avoid the turtle-eating alligator that lives there? This is a readers theatre script for six players.

Set

Three stools are arranged on one side of the stage, with space in the front for the alligator to sit on the floor. Two more stools are grouped together on the other side of the stage.

Props

No props are required.

Costumes

No costumes are required.

Characters

Narrator
Willie
Frank
Max
Mrs. Crow
Crunch

THE THREE SNAPPING TURTLES

Narrator: My name is _____. I play the Narrator.

Willie: *(High voice.)* My name is _____. I play the youngest snapping turtle. My brothers call me Willie.

Frank: *(Medium voice.)* My name is _____. I play the middle snapping turtle. My brothers call me Frank.

Max: *(Deep voice.)* My name is _____. I play the oldest snapping turtle. My brothers call me Max.

Mrs. Crow: *(Squeaky voice.)* My name is _____. I play Mrs. Crow.

Crunch: *(Gravelly voice.)* My name is _____. I play a hungry alligator. My friends call me Crunch.

(Characters go to their stools and sit. Crunch sits on the floor.)

Narrator: All right then, let's begin. Once upon a time, three turtles needed a new pond. The oldest went looking for one, while the other two stayed behind.

Willie: How long has Max been gone now, Frank?

Frank: Two minutes longer than the last time you asked, Willie.

Willie: Yeah, but he's still not back and I'm worried.

Frank: Worrying won't bring him home any sooner.

Willie: Can't we go look for him?

Frank: He told us to wait here. If we leave he won't be able to find us.

Willie: What if he's lost or hurt?

Frank: All right, all right. Let's climb up the bank and take a look on the other side. *(Pauses.)*

Willie: I see a beaver dam. Do beavers eat turtles?

Frank: They only eat turtles that ask too many questions.

Willie: I have only one more question: Do you see Max?

Frank: Nope, but I think I know why our pond dried up. Those beavers blocked the river.

Willie: Rotten beavers. I hope Max comes home soon. I'm hungry.

Frank: I am too.

Narrator: The two turtles chewed the last water lily leaf left in their pond while they watched for their brother. Meanwhile, Max met a crow. She was perched on a fallen tree that spanned a river.

Max: Excuse me, Mrs. Crow. Do you live around here?

Mrs. Crow: *(Crabby.)* Of course I do. Is there a law against it?

Max: I didn't mean to pry, but you could have been just passing through.

Mrs. Crow: Well, I *am* just passing through, boy. I'm passing through while I look for twigs for my new nest.

Max: Do you know whether there are any fresh ponds on the other side of this river?

Mrs. Crow: Yes, there are.

Max: How close are they?

Mrs. Crow: You mean as a crow flies or as a turtle plods?

Max: *(Sighs.)* As a turtle plods, ma'am.

Mrs. Crow: I guess it would take *you* part of a morning to climb the bank to the other side. There's a pond right there.

Max: That close, huh. Thank you ma'am. By the way, there's an alligator under that log and he's been watching you.

Mrs. Crow: He must like my shiny black feathers. Helloooo. Mr. Alligator?

Crunch: Yes?

Mrs. Crow: Is there something I can do for you sir or are you just jealous of my beautiful feathers?

Crunch: I'd be able to admire them better if I could see them more clearly. Care to come closer?

Narrator: Crunch had a very hungry look on his face.

Mrs. Crow: Do I look like I was born yesterday? I see your big teeth.

Crunch: Uh, yeah, they are fine, aren't they? That's why my friends call me Crunch.

Narrator: While Crunch said this, he gave his broad tail a mighty swish and shot out of the river toward the log.

Max: Watch out! He's going to ram your log!

Narrator: Crunch bumped the log with his long snout, hoping the crow would fall into his waiting jaws.

Mrs. Crow: AAAWWWK! I must be going . . . things to do, places to go. Ta, ta. Caw, caw, caw . . .

Narrator: Mrs. Crow flew off, while Crunch turned his hungry gaze on the large snapping turtle on the bank.

Crunch: Rats. Foiled again, but I can still enjoy a tasty turtle.

Max: Not today . . . I have things to do, too. Ta, ta.

Narrator: Max the turtle moved out of sight.

Crunch: Hey, where's everybody going? Was it something I said?

Narrator: Max went home. The next morning the brothers set off for their new pond. They had a plan. When the three snapping turtles got to the river, Willie went first. As he stepped onto the log, Crunch appeared.

Crunch: Yum. A tasty turtle for breakfast.

Willie: Maybe so, but I'm very skinny. My brother, Frank, is right behind me and he's meatier. Why don't you wait for him?

Crunch: Why don't I *not* wait and just eat you now?

Willie: Because if you eat me, Frank will see and then *he* won't cross. You'll still be hungry.

Crunch: I suppose you're right. Okay, I'll wait.

Narrator: Once Willie got close to the other side, Frank started across the log.

Crunch: Oh, boy. Looks like I get a two for one deal this morning.

Frank: Good morning, Mr. Crunch. May I make a suggestion?

Crunch: Like don't eat you? Funny, I've heard that before.

Frank: You must not be very hungry then.

Crunch: No, I'm not, I'm just starving.

Frank: Then why settle for two turtles when you can have three?

Crunch: Wait, I know this one . . . because there *are* only two?

Frank: Sure, right now, but Max is coming.

Crunch: I've heard of sibling rivalry, but you boys win a prize. Why don't I just invite you down into my river for a nice cool swim and a little game of tag?

Narrator: As you can guess, he meant to tag those turtles with his teeth.

Frank: Sounds like fun. Wait just a few minutes and Max will show up. I'm sure he'll want to play, too.

Narrator: Frank lumbered onto the log while Crunch licked his lips. When he got to the middle of the log, he stopped and waited for Max's signal.

Max: Ready, get set, go!

Narrator: Frank and Willie jumped onto Crunch's back and snapped their strong jaws onto his tail.

Crunch: Yow! Let go! That hurts!

Narrator: Max laughed and said—

Max: Tag you're it.

Narrator: Max jumped into the river and bit Crunch's tail too. Crunch thrashed around and bit at those turtles, but he couldn't shake them off. Finally he decided to smash them against the riverbank. He swung his tail out of the water toward the bank. The three snapping turtles let go of the tail as they sailed toward the riverbank.

Max, Frank, Willie: Wheeee! Oooof!

Narrator: They each landed safely on the other side. Crunch watched with his mouth hanging wide open.

Max: Still have a taste for turtles?

Frank: . . . Especially if they're at bargain prices?

Willie: . . . And they can beat you at tag?

Crunch: *(Moans.)* Oh, my poor tail. I'll never eat turtles again. They're way too much trouble. I never did like the taste, anyway. They taste like chicken.

Narrator: After that day, Crunch found another tree for shade and the three snapping turtles never saw him again. They found three new ponds full of fish. Mrs. Crow visited once in a while.

Mrs. Crow: You boys haven't seen any juicy worms around here, have you? You ever try feeding six baby crows? They're bottomless.

Narrator: Willie had an idea.

Willie: Maybe that fisherman would let you have some. He has a whole bucketful, ma'am.

Narrator: And that is the story of how three turtles crossed a river, defeated an alligator, and met their new neighbor in a pond near a river through a forest. The end.

5

Fairy Tale Variations for Plays

Story Adaptation

In this chapter a fairy tale will be altered again, but this time it will be turned into a play. As in Chapter 3, the ground rules for staging the play will have to be set according to what is available at the school. Urge students to be creative with "found things," a skill that will be very useful as students pursue their new-found interest in theater.

In Chapter 4 students saw how changing billy goats into turtles led to all sorts of adjustments. On a bigger scale, we will take all the characters in the story of "Snow White and the Seven Dwarves" and place them in New York City during the Great Depression. Where might there be a young girl and seven other people who could interact like the originals, not to mention an evil stepmother, a deceased father, and a handsome prince?

If the castle becomes a restaurant and hotel right on Central Park, the stepmother could become a mean and demanding owner. For fun, we could call the restaurant the Magic Mirror. The seven dwarves could be chefs, while Snow White could be a daughter who must work in the kitchen because her father has died and left her stepmother in charge of her inheritance—the restaurant.

The main character, based on Snow White, can have a name that still starts with "S" as a clue to the reader—perhaps Sally. Giving the imagination free rein, we can create seven characters with names similar to the dwarves and have fun with alliteration. For instance, Doc could become Doctor Dave who is in charge of drinks, making the best lemonade in town. Sleepy could become Sleepy Sue in charge of soups. What makes her sleepy? She has a new baby at home who keeps her awake at night, so Sue sometimes dozes off while stirring her soups. Bashful Bob is a baker who has tremendously strong arms from kneading bread, but he's shy. Sneezy Louise prepares the peas, sometimes with onions, sometimes with lemon or mushrooms, but always with pepper. Happy Huey loves grilling his famous hamburgers with a variety of toppings. Grumpy Gus is a graham cracker-crust pie specialist who can't take criticism. He even suspects praise is sarcastic, which adds to his grumpiness. Finally, there is the dishwasher named Dan who is a war veteran with an iron plate in his skull and who got his job through his friend Doctor Dave. That doesn't sound dopey at all, even though there is great alliteration with Dopey Dan the dishwasher. What if Dan loves to joke around, claiming the plate in his skull is the only one he knows that never needs scrubbing? His favorite joke is to tap the metal plate with a wooden spoon and make faces at the bus boys who bring him more dirty dishes. The new story has a playful tone.

How do we include the prince and evil stepmother? What if Sally recognizes a restaurant critic (the prince) from his picture in the newspaper and gives him the best table in the house? The next day his column praises all of the specialty chefs and especially the friendly and beautiful hostess (Sally), while completely ignoring the owner (the evil stepmother), who becomes very jealous. Sally is fired. The action is similar to the original story, but the names and places have been changed. Can the characters live happily ever after? Is there a twist?

Playwriting

The "Snow White" plot is complicated and has many characters and several settings. This story demands a full play script, where actors in seventh or eighth grade can wear simple costumes and use props, while others create sets, run lights, and maybe even choose musical scores. If there are enough actors available, more can be used as extras in the kitchen and as patrons in the restaurant. Keep things simple to allow for minimal budgets.

Regular plays rarely use narrators, so the characters' dialog and actions must tell the story. Begin with a list of characters and a sentence to indicate the setting. The beginning scene must tell the main conflict in the story: What is the problem and why do we care about the characters? Let the background information filter through the conversation. Perhaps a confrontation with the stepmother would get things rolling.

In Scene 2, Sally can be shown working among the kitchen staff, thus introducing those characters. The audience is introduced to the conflict in the story in Scene 1 and then is relieved by comedy as the characters with their silly names are introduced. Don't let the audience become complacent just because they think they know the story; keep them guessing. There are many problems in this story, from the setting during the Depression to mean bosses. It could get gloomy as problems arise if characters are unsuccessful in overcoming them. By giving our chefs playful names, we have a vehicle for comic relief.

Scene 3 can introduce the critic, an element of hope. In Scene 4 the jealous stepmother fires Sally. Suspense builds. In Scene 5 the problems are solved, because after all, fairy tales always have happy endings . . . or do they? Notice how the alliteration in the title hints at more fun to come. See *Sally's Seven Chefs* on the next page to see how this version turns out.

SALLY'S SEVEN CHEFS

Summary

Sally's stepmother runs the Magic Mirror restaurant in New York City during the Depression. Sally's father has died so Sally must work for her mean stepmother. A restaurant critic changes their lives. This is a play for thirteen characters plus extras.

Set

Set the whole stage at the beginning. Stage lights are turned on and off to change the scene between one side (the kitchen) and the other (the restaurant). A couple of long tables identify the kitchen. A potted tree defines the entrance to the restaurant, and a table with a tablecloth, small flower vase, and three chairs are the restaurant. A music stand is the hostess station. Change the tablecloth and flowers for Scene 5 to represent a different restaurant. Depending on how many extras are available, they can be busboys, waiters, and diners at additional tables.

Props

Sally needs a grocery list, basket, and a menu; Sue needs a soup pot and ladle; Bob needs a breadboard and perhaps Play-Doh to knead. Dave needs a pitcher with ice cubes and a bowl of cut lemons. Louise needs a saucepan and spoon. Dan needs a dishpan, soap suds, and a wooden spoon. Gus needs pie pans. Huey needs a skillet with hamburgers and a spatula. Food can either be mimed or plastic. Mrs. Morse can look studious with reading glasses, and Frances the maid carries a feather duster. Bus boys use plastic dish pans. Waiters need small towels to drape over their arms, plus pads of paper and pens.

Costumes

Mrs. Morse and Mrs. Warner wear dresses. Frances wears a maid's cap and white apron. Chef's hats or bandanas to cover hair and aprons can be the costumes for all the chefs. Sally wears jeans in the kitchen scene but dresses up as the hostess. Karl wears a jacket and tie, and Joseph wears a white shirt, dress pants, and a tie. Bus boys are in jeans and white shirts.

Characters

Mrs. Morse *(nanny)*   Karl Prince *(a restaurant critic)*
Frances *(maid)*   Joseph the waiter
Mrs. Warner *(Sally's stepmother)*   Dopey Dan
Sally Warner   Doctor Dave

Sleepy Sue					Sneezy Louise
Bashful Bob					Happy Huey
							Grumpy Gus

Extras: busboys, waiters, restaurant patrons

SALLY'S SEVEN CHEFS

Scene 1—The Magic Mirror Restaurant in Manhattan

(Lights rise on two well-dressed ladies and a maid at a table in the restaurant.)

Mrs. Warner: Mrs. Morse and my dear Frances, I'm afraid I have some disturbing news.

Frances: Oh, my. I knew it was bad news when you asked us both to come.

Mrs. Morse: Now Frances, you mustn't always expect the worst. I assume, Mrs. Warner, you are satisfied with my performance as Miss Sally's tutor?

Mrs. Warner: I am perfectly happy with your performance, Mrs. Morse. Unfortunately, I find myself in the difficult position of having insufficient funds to continue your salary.

Frances: Oh, please don't let me go, Mrs. Warner. I have no place else to go. I will work for you for free if I can keep my garret room and take meals downstairs with the kitchen staff. Please, Mrs. Warner?

Mrs. Warner: Well, I would never suggest such a thing; that would be slavery. Besides, you're forgetting your aunt across the river. You could live there.

Frances: Oh, no. Please don't make me go back there. She has seven children; all of them beasts, and none of them do a lick of work. I would rather be out on the streets standing in bread lines than go there.

Mrs. Warner: Well, if you insist. I suppose you could remain in your room and take your meals downstairs, but I'm afraid I cannot afford to pay you.

Frances: That's all right. Thank you, Mrs. Warner. You won't be sorry. I'll still be the best maid you've ever had.

Mrs. Warner: In that case, you may be excused to finish your dusting. Also, the front parlor rugs all require a good beating, and the silver candlesticks are in an atrocious state of tarnish. See to them as well.

Frances: Yes, ma'am. Thank you, ma'am. Excuse me, Mrs. Morse. *(Exits.)*

Mrs. Morse: I suppose you are going to offer me the same ridiculous terms as that poor silly girl, so I will save you the trouble. My two weeks' notice begins today.

Mrs. Warner: You are only required to give one week's notice, Mrs. Morse, and I would be happy to consider it retroactive to last week.

Mrs. Morse: Of course you would, because that would save you the trouble of giving me another week's pay, but I've read my contract and know my rights. I will expect my pay in two weeks. Good day, Mrs. Warner. *(Stands to leave.)*

Mrs. Warner: I do hope you understand that my reduced circumstances have forced me to do this, Mrs. Morse. I know you were good friends with my late husband, and I hope we can continue to be friends.

Mrs. Morse: I understand nothing of the sort. I do, however, understand that you have always been jealous of the kindness your husband showed me out of respect for my work, that your circumstances are no more reduced than the President's, that it is impossible to continue to be friends with someone with whom I have never been friends, and that you wish to have me gone so that you can treat your daughter as another slave.

Mrs. Warner: That will be all, Mrs. Morse. You will leave at once.

Mrs. Morse: Yes I will, but if I do not receive my salary, you will hear from my solicitor. In addition, keep in mind that I will be watching you and will do everything in my power to protect Miss Sally from your malice. Now, if you will excuse me . . .

Mrs. Warner: Do not expect me to cower at your feet, Mrs. Morse. I, too, have solicitors and may find it necessary to place a restraining order on your contact with my daughter.

Mrs. Morse: Do so at your own risk, Madam. Good Day. *(Exits. Lights down.)*

Scene 2—The Kitchen of the Magic Mirror

(Lights rise as all chefs enter and work in kitchen. Enter Sally.)

Sally: Good morning, everyone. I'm heading to the market, so please let me know what you will need. I'll come around to all of you before I leave. I'll start with you, Sleepy Sue. How's the baby?

Sue: He kept me up all night, Miss. He's colicky.

Sally: I'm so sorry, Sue. Is there anything I can do?

Sue: You're sweet to ask, Deary, but there's nothing me and my Hal ain't tried. The doctor says he'll grow out of it in a few months.

Sally: Your Hal is a prince, Sue. He'll see you through, I'm sure, but if you need to lie down once your soup is simmering, you may use my room anytime, okay?

Sue: Yes, Miss. Thank you. As for my groceries: I need more carrots, a bag of potatoes, some onions, and cream.

Sally: Fine. And how about you, Doctor Dan? How is your supply of lemons?

Dan: Last I looked, there was still a bushel in the cellar. I could use more of my secret ingredient for the lemonade, though.

Sally: Ah yes, say no more. Your secret is safe with me. Our customers love to guess how you doctor your drinks. They've guessed everything from cough syrup to molasses.

Dan: They'll never guess, and I'd never tell. It keeps them coming back for more.

Sally: I'll check the cellar on my way out. We wouldn't want to run out of your lemonade. It is in great demand these days because of the heat. We have to keep the customers satisfied, right?

Dan: You bet. Thank you, Miss.

Sally: Good morning, Louise. How will you be preparing your peas today?

Louise: Oh, well, let me . . . see . . . aachoo!

Sally: Bless you, Sneezy.

Louise: Thank you . . . aaa . . . aaa . . . *(Sniffs.)* False alarm. I think I would like to try adding some of those tiny white onions, if you can still get them, Miss. They make such a lovely dish.

Sally: Tiny onions. Okay, I'll look for them. I think I know just the vendor to ask, too. Remember Mr. Reed? He's always asking after you and often adds extras to your requests. I think he's sweet on you, Louise.

Louise: Oh, no. I don't think so, Sally. He's way too handsome to notice a plain girl like me.

Sally: Oh, he notices you all right. Maybe you should come with me and purchase your own onions, just to see for yourself.

Louise: Mrs. Warner would have my head if she thought I was fraternizing with the produce man, Miss Sally, you know that. Just tell Mr. Reed "Hi" for me, will you?

Sally: Certainly. Oh, there you are, Gus. Will you need anything for your pies?

Gus: I was going to make lemon meringue, but Doc won't share the lemons. I overheard Sue asking for cream, so why don't you get extra and some eggs and bananas for me. I guess I'll just have to make banana cream pie, not that anyone will eat it.

Sally: Banana cream pie? What a great idea, Grumpy. We haven't offered that for weeks. I'm sure our customers will be lining up in the street for that.

Gus: Oh, sure, they'll be lining up in the streets. We'll look like a soup kitchen and that will drive away all our paying customers. I'll lose my job, the restaurant will close, the hotel will go bust . . .

Sally: Well, I know it will be a hit, Gus. I'll feature it on our menu board in the lobby.

Gus: My luck, everyone will fill up on dinner so they don't have room for dessert anyway.

Sally: Maybe, but you know our late-night theater patrons always want dessert with coffee. Don't worry, it'll be gone by tomorrow.

Gus: That's what I love about this job. Nothing lasts. . . . Oh, don't forget butter for the graham cracker crusts. The customers demand them, and since they're always right . . .

Sally: Butter, okay. Cheer up, Gus. I'd better move before everything's picked over at the market. How about you, Bashful? You need anything for your breads?

Bob: *Knead* anything? Sure I do, like this potato bread, that wheat bread, those dinner rolls . . . oh, you mean *need*. No, thank you. I'm all set.

Sally: And . . . heeere's Huey the Hamburger baron. What toppings are you going to need, Huey?

Huey: Hi, Sally. Pretty broach you have there. You look lovely this morning, like a million bucks. Toppings, huh? How about some mushrooms, cheese, and some tomatoes if they look fresh, okay?

Sally: *(Writes it down.)* Fresh tomatoes only, mushrooms, cheese—cheddar?

Huey: Cheddar, provolone, swiss, doesn't matter. Whatever looks best. Thanks, darlin'.

Sally: My pleasure. Hey, Huey, have you seen Dan?

Huey: Sure, he's over there boiling water for the dishes. Why?

Sally: It's his birthday today, you know, and . . . *(She's interrupted by a drumroll made by wooden spoons on metal pots.)*

Dan: *(Sings.)* Happy birthday to me, happy birthday . . .

Sally: Come on everybody; sing with me. We can't have Dopey Dan singing his birthday song all by himself. *(They all finish the song.)*

Everyone: *(Shouts.)* Happy Birthday, Dan! *(Dan makes faces at everyone, and then takes a bow.)*

Sally: *(To Doctor Dave.)* Gee, Doc. Isn't that the third time this week it was Dan's birthday?

Dave: *(Whispers.)* Yep, but it sure gets him off to a great start. I wonder if his war wounds are bothering him, you know, like the metal plate in his head. I'll talk with him.

Dan: I heard that. Don't worry about me; I'm fine. I just like to sing and it's the only song I can remember. Besides, I thought it got the whole kitchen off to a great start.

Dave: Well it does, old friend, and we all appreciate your sense of humor.

Dan: Not everyone does. Did you see that new bus boy yesterday? I did my usual performance, you know, tapping my head with a spoon and saying "It's the only plate I know that doesn't need washing." He looked at me like I had rabies. I even made googly eyes at him to prove I was joking.

Dave: You're right. I met him. No sense of humor. Maybe we should make tomorrow his birthday.

Dan: Great idea.

Sally: Bye all. I'm on my way, unless you can think of anything else?

(Room hushes as Mrs. Warner enters.)

Mrs. Warner: Think about getting back to work before you all have to think about getting new jobs. What are you doing here still, Sally? You should have left thirty minutes ago. You'll get nothing but rotten scraps if you don't go now.

Sally: Yes, mother. I'm going. *(Exits.)*

Gus: *(Mutters.)* As if she's expected to buy the best on pennies.

Mrs. Warner: What's that, Gus?

Gus: Nothing, ma'am.

Mrs. Warner: Any more grumbling from you and you can follow Mrs. Morse right on out of here, mister.

Gus: Yes, ma'am. Sorry, ma'am.

Mrs. Warner: Well? What are you all standing around for? I'm not paying you to stand around. Cook something! *(Spins around and leaves. Lights down.)*

Scene 3—A Late Diner

(Louise is in the kitchen, but the lights are dim. Other chefs come and go quietly. Lights up on restaurant. Sally is behind the hostess stand. Enter Karl.)

Sally: I'm sorry, sir, we were just about to close. *(Hesitates, then recognizes him.)* Oh, welcome Mr. Prince. We're always open for you.

Karl: How kind, Miss. Have we met?

Sally: No, but I recognize you from your picture in the paper. You're the restaurant critic, aren't you?

Karl: Yes, you're right, but please keep it under your hat. I'd like a small table near the kitchen so I can have a nice, quiet supper.

Sally: I understand, sir. Follow me, please. *(Shows him to the table and hands him a menu.)* Would you like to hear our specials tonight?

Karl: Yes, go ahead.

Sally: We have a creamy vegetable soup, mushroom cheddar hamburgers, fresh scrod with lemons, which are accompanied very well with fresh-squeezed lemonade and peas with tiny, sweet onions. For dessert we have banana cream pie. I'll give you a moment while I get you some bread.

Karl: Thank you. *(Sally goes into the kitchen.)*

Sally: Hey, Louise. Pass the word. We have a special guest tonight. Karl Prince, the food critic from the *New York Tribune* is here. Let's give him our best.

Louise: Yes, Miss. I'll pass it around. Thanks. *(Sally leaves with a basket of bread.)*

Sally: Here you go, Mr. Prince.

Karl: Thank you, Miss. *(Looks in the basket.)* Mmm, these look good. Are they baked here? *(Takes a bite.)*

Sally: Yes, Mr. Prince. Bob has been baking our breads for ten years. We're very proud of him.

Karl: Bob's baked breads are the best! This is delicious.

Sally: *(Laughs.)* Thank you. Oh, here you are Joseph. Mr. Prince, this is Joseph and he will be your waiter tonight. Take good care of Mr. Prince, Joseph. Excuse me. *(Exits.)*

Joseph: Yes, ma'am. Are you ready to order, sir?

Karl: Yes, please bring me every one of your specials.

Joseph: Certainly, sir. Would you like a cup or a bowl of our creamy vegetable soup?

Karl: A cup would be fine.

Joseph: As you wish. *(Goes into kitchen and returns with cup.)* How may we fix your hamburger, sir?

Karl: Medium.

Joseph: Excellent. And do you wish to have the hamburger served with the scrod and peas?

Karl: Yes, all at once.

Joseph: Very good, sir. *(Exits. Enter Sally.)*

Sally: Oh, good. I see you've already been served. If you need anything, just ask for Sally, okay?

Karl: Only if you'll call me Karl. Have you closed the front doors yet?

Sally: Yes, just now. How did you know?

Karl: Just a lucky guess. In that case, won't you sit down and join me? I don't like eating alone.

Sally: I'm not allowed to sit with our customers, sir. I'm sorry. Is your soup all right?

Karl: Delicious. If you cannot join me, then I shall have to invite you to dinner another evening. May I?

Sally: That would be delightful. *(Enter Joseph with Karl's supper.)* Ah, good. There you are. I'll leave you to your meal.

Karl: When can I call on you?

Sally: We close early tomorrow night.

Karl: Then I will come around for you at closing time tomorrow. Agreed?

Sally: I look forward to it. *(Exits. Lights down.)*

Scene 4—The Restaurant Review

(Lights up on kitchen. It is morning. Gus and Louise are working. Others enter as the scene continues. Enter Mrs. Warner.)

Mrs. Warner: Louise, where's Sally?

Louise: Aaaah . . . aaah . . .

Mrs. Warner: Don't you dare sneeze, Louise. I demand you stop this instant. It's disgusting and unsanitary.

Louise: Aaaah . . . aaah . . .

Mrs. Warner: One sneeze and you're fired.

Louise: Chooo!

Mrs. Warner: That's it. Hand me your apron and get out of my kitchen. *(Exit Louise, sniffling.)* Gus, tell me where Sally is hiding or you're next.

Gus: But Mrs. Warner, I have no . . .

Mrs. Warner: Of course you know where she is; now out with it. I must speak with her immediately.

Gus: But . . . *(Enter Sally, carrying baskets of groceries.)*

Mrs. Warner: There you are, you sniveling little brat. What did you do, spend the whole night flirting shamelessly with that restaurant critic? He featured the Magic Mirror this morning, and your name was mentioned ten times. Do you know how many times he mentioned the beautiful and elegant owner?

Sally: No, Mother. I haven't had time to . . .

Mrs. Warner: Read the paper? Of course not; I don't pay you to read the paper.

Gus: *(Mumbles.)* You don't pay her at all.

Mrs. Warner: *(Spins around to face Gus.)* How dare you. You're fired. Get out of my kitchen now. *(Exit Gus.)*

Sally: But Mother, we need . . .

Mrs. Warner: Don't "but Mother" me, and we certainly don't need insolent cooks. He's replaceable. As for that critic, did I tell you my name never came up? I've never been so insulted in my life. I will not tolerate your behavior another second. Pack your things and leave at once. I never want to see your face again. *(Everyone in the kitchen freezes—there is absolute silence.)*

Sally: As you wish, Stepmother. I'm sorry if . . .

Mrs. Warner: You're not sorry and there are no "ifs" about it. You're finished around here. You don't deserve my charity and you won't get any sympathy either. You're an ungrateful, insensitive, self-serving little brat. Now get out! *(Exit Sally. Kitchen activity resumes feverishly.)* That's right, get back to work or you'll all be out on the street. *(Exits, lights dim.)*

Scene 5—Martin's on the Park

(Lights up on a different restaurant table. Karl and Sally are having coffee.)

Karl: Well, Sally. You have certainly proven yourself around here over the last few weeks. You managed to staff the new kitchen, decorate the restaurant, train the new waiters, and design a menu that is drawing crowds every night.

Sally: I've loved every minute of it, Karl. Thank you for introducing me to the owner.

Karl: It was my pleasure. I've known Martin for years, and I knew he'd need help with this new hotel and restaurant.

Sally: I wish you'd seen their faces when I offered mother's chefs a job here. They all dropped everything and walked out immediately.

Karl: Are all of them here now? I bet you'll hear from her lawyers soon.

Sally: I already have, but she has no case. They had every right to leave.

Karl: You don't think I was too hard on her, do you? I mean my article may well have finished her off.

Sally: She never did take criticism well. It wasn't your fault that she couldn't hire anyone decent, including bus boys or a cleaning crew. For her, employee means the same as slave. People need to be treated with dignity, especially during this Depression. It's all some people have left.

Karl: You're right. I'm also very impressed with your idea to house the staff right here in the hotel. When will the renovations to their apartments be finished?

Sally: Very soon. They loved choosing their own paint colors and carpeting. The nursery for Sue and Louise's children is getting a mural. They won't have to worry about their children wandering the streets as long as Mrs. Morse is in charge.

Karl: Are there any of the original staff left at the Magic Mirror?

Sally: Only the doorman.

Karl: Poor guy, but he was a sour puss. She deserves him. Martin's location is more desirable. Central Park is right outside your front door and the theater is only a few blocks away. Gus' pies draw crowds.

Sally: Gus is a genius. Have you tried his new key lime pie?

Karl: Yes, I just finished mine before you came over. All I know is, this is my new favorite choice for our wedding dessert.

Sally: Our what?

Karl: You heard me. What do you say? Can you fit a wedding into your schedule for . . . say . . . next Tuesday?

Sally: Oh, Karl . . . I mean yes, I do, I *will* marry you and I *can* clear my schedule for Tuesday. *(Hops out of chair and throws arms around Karl. Lights dim.)*

Fairy Tale Variations for Plays

Other Stories to Adapt

"Goldilocks and the Three Bears"

"Hansel and Gretel"

"Jack and the Beanstalk"

"The Three Little Pigs"

"The Ugly Duckling"

"Cinderella"

"City Mouse–Country Mouse"

Or consider stories by Hans Christian Andersen, The Brothers Grimm, and Mother Goose.

Extensions

1. Plan a performance contest between classes, where each one adapts the same fairy tale and then they all perform for the same audience of younger schoolmates, who vote for their favorite. The prize can be a week without homework for the winning team.

2. Assign projects to nonactors such as:
   - Designing and painting set backdrops onto donated plain white sheets.
   - Gathering costumes and props.
   - Running the lights.
   - Designing a musical score from collected tapes or CDs, or performing a musical piece.
   - Writing and printing up programs.

6

Modern Fairy Tale Plays

Story Adaptation

There are so many ways to use familiar fairy tales to inspire creative writing. In previous chapters we created a choral reading, a readers theatre script, and plays. For this chapter we will take the story of "Hansel and Gretel," a story set in the mythical past of "once upon a time," and change it to create a modern story. This is a great exercise for exploring any modern culture. Using the bones or plot of a fairy tale and placing it within another culture forces students to consider the effects of the differences they find while realizing that some things are still the same. Rather than merely reading about a culture, students stretch their imaginations to identify with the people.

The theme of "Hansel and Gretel" is multilayered. It tells of poverty, cruelty, selfishness, and wickedness, all of which leave the heroes of the story—Hansel and Gretel—only slightly shaken in their hope and love for each other. All of these themes are universal; they are found in all places and all times. Can we transform the characters into modern ones? Will the theme still work for a modern tale, or is it necessary to adjust the problems as well?

Consider the fairy tales mentioned at the end of Chapter 5: "Goldilocks and the Three Bears," "Hansel and Gretel," "Jack and the Beanstalk," "The Three Little Pigs," "The Ugly Duckling," "Cinderella," and "City Mouse–Country Mouse." Out of seven stories, four feature anthropomorphic animals. Modern children, especially those in third through eighth grades, are not interested in animal stories. However, they are old enough to realize that the animals represent people and that appearances and stereotypes can be misleading.

For instance, ask a class to turn the three little pigs into western pioneers and see what happens. The students might develop a story about the different reactions of three brothers when they first encounter wolves out west. One brother might hide under a bush and be eaten, another might run to a log cabin and wait for the wolves to leave. A third would run to the trading post for protection. Each is afraid, just like the pigs, and each makes a choice. How the story ends will depend on the wolves and the writer. Is this story about man versus beast and survival of the fittest? Perhaps it will be told from the perspective of the hungry pack of wolves needing to protect young pups and feed them.

What will students learn from this exercise? As with the chapters in this book that use poetry to inspire plays, the fairy tales provide a framework, a hanger for the clothing of the play. Students take the clothing down, try it on, alter it, and hang it back up. Their new fashions are original plays.

The original Hansel and Gretel are poor German children living with their evil stepmother and loving though henpecked father. Unfortunately, terrible parents can be found all over the world today, just as poor children are common. If the story were set in a country such as China or Guatemala, students would need to research those cultures before they could see how to adapt the story. For instance, perhaps instead of a witch and a gingerbread house, the children in China would find a dragon and his stolen treasure, or Guatemalan children might find a Mayan demon and his poisonous maize.

What if two elements were changed, for instance, by making the family wealthy, and keeping all the characters in the same roles but placing them in a modern setting. What kind of scenario would accommodate the story elements and the two changes? If the modern children are spoiled and rich, what other changes might happen in the story? Perhaps the father is aloof because he works long hours and the mother is resentful because her children refuse to do their chores. If the gingerbread house and witch represent overcoming greed and working together in the original story, what can modern wealthy children do that is similar? Perhaps a gingerbread house can still play a role as the children find it in their attic, devour most of it, and then must face up to their mother for spoiling her party centerpiece.

This kind of adaptation becomes even more creative with input from a team, so that is how students should be divided. Small groups of three or five work best, because an odd number of students in each group creates an automatic tie-breaker when it comes to making key decisions. The best part about this exercise is the way ideas build on each other, with one brilliant twist leading to another.

Playwriting

Depending on the creative energy within the group, it may be necessary to help the students focus by giving them a list of leading questions, such as those at the beginning of Chapter 3. A simplified list follows:

1. What happens if you change the beginning of the fairy tale? The middle? The end?

2. What if a different character becomes the main one? How does the story change?

3. What if the story happens in another place? Another time?

4. What if the antagonist is the protagonist (bad guy becomes the good guy)?

5. What if the antagonist tells the story? What would change? Would he still be bad?

Once students have decided which part of a story they wish to change, they can use the planning sheet included at the end of this chapter. Notice the four large boxes that will help students keep track of the story elements and how they will change in the new version. Once the decisions are made, perhaps done by using the clustering technique, a summary paragraph will help guide the action for the script. There is only a small space provided because students must really focus their story in a summary and not get bogged down in details.

However, it is still important to consider those details so that they can be noted under the additional headings like stage, furniture, props, costumes, and lights. A middle school drama class will have the means to plan and create more elaborate sets and costumes while younger classes should pool the resources of art and "specials" teachers as well as enlist the aid of a parent volunteer or team of volunteers to help line up donations and borrowed items. The following sample demonstrates how the decisions affect each other and create an outline for an original story. (A blank version, Form 6.1, appears at the end of this chapter.)

Script Adaptation Sheet

1. What fairy tale will you adapt? *Hansel and Gretel*

2. List story elements	**3. List revised elements**
selfish stepmother, loving father, poor	*loving mother, busy father, rich*
loving children who stick together	*spoiled children, selfish*
gingerbread house/wicked witch	*gingerbread house*
cunning escape	*trapped by greed*
reunion with father, happy family	*remorseful children, new understanding*

4. List characters	**5. Rename characters**
Hansel	*Henry*
Gretel	*Gretchen*
Father	*Dad*
Stepmother	*Mom*
Wicked Witch	

6. Write a summary of the modernized story. *Henry and Gretchen are spoiled rich kids. Their mother is determined to teach them responsibility, but they refuse to cooperate. The day before their Christmas party, the children hide in the attic and eat a whole wall of the party's gingerbread house. They complain about sick stomachs. Their mother suspects flu and decides to cancel the party. Fearing the loss of presents, the kids help clean up the house. Their mother finds the eaten gingerbread house and is very upset, but the kids salvage it. In the end, they've enjoyed working together.*

7. Stage Design: Is a backdrop needed? *No. Scene 1, attic and candy house can be created with empty boxes and stacked furniture from teacher's lounge set up to divide the attic from the dining room area. Gingerbread houses (one whole, one eaten) donated by local grocer or ambitious moms. Scene 3, dining room has table and chairs.*

8. List furniture required. *Cardboard boxes, lamp, dining room table, chairs.*

9. List actors/costumes needed. *Henry and Gretchen wear play clothes. Gretchen wears a winter coat in Scene 3. Mom and Dad wear casual clothes, Mom has a bandana in her hair, father needs a winter coat, apron.*

10. List the props. *Ten empty cardboard boxes of various sizes, a lamp, gingerbread house, tablecloth, party plates, and silverware.*

11. How many stage hands are needed, and what are their jobs? *None needed. Stage will be split so that the attic is on one side, the dining room on the other, all set up at the beginning of the play.*

12. Are stage lights available? Decide what will cue the lights. *Yes, lights will rise at the beginning, only half lit on attic side, switching to other as children move. Lights dim after final bow.*

13. Are there sound effects? Will they be live or recorded? Cue sounds? *No.*

14. Write a description of the opening scene. *Henry and Gretchen hide in the attic to avoid their chores. They discover the gingerbread house and help themselves. They are sad at the loss of their grandmother who used to bake these.*

Notice that in box 2 of the Script Adaptation Sheet the elements of the story are merely key words. In box 3, opposites match each item of box 2. The names of the children are modern and the wicked witch is gone because the children have become the antagonists. No longer is it necessary to escape from the witch; now the children must escape their own greed and selfishness. Little is left of the original story, except for perhaps the similarity in the names of the children and the candy house.

The final decision is where to begin the action of the play. A moment must be found that will grab the audience's interest. A scene where the children hide in the attic eating the gingerbread house shows how Henry and Gretchen think and act. If done right, the scene will create a tension—will they get caught? Will they pay for hiding from their chores? Since we've decided Henry and Gretchen are naughty, it is important to make the audience sympathetic to them. Like all good characters, they must have redeeming qualities to round out their flaws. Simply naughty children are predictable, but children who have second thoughts might change and make better decisions. The tension and sympathy comes as the audience watches the characters struggle with their decisions. Take a look at *The Secret of Success*.

THE SECRET OF SUCCESS

Summary

Henry and Gretchen have everything they need, including a Christmas party planned for tomorrow. Why did their mom lock the attic? Will the children spoil their surprise or will they find something wonderful?

Sets

An attic is created with empty boxes stacked to divide the attic area from the dining room area of the stage. The dining room has a long table and chairs.

Props

Ten cardboard boxes, a lamp, two gingerbread houses (one to eat, one repaired), tablecloth, party plates, and silverware.

Costumes

Henry and Gretchen wear play clothes, Mom wears casual clothes, Mom has a bandana in her hair. Gretchen and Dad need winter coats for Scene 3 and Dad needs an apron for Scene 3.

Characters

Gretchen
Henry
Mom
Dad

THE SECRET OF SUCCESS

Scene 1—The Attic

(As lights rise, Henry and Gretchen enter attic area, brushing off their hands and pants.)

Gretchen: We shouldn't have come up here, Henry. This place is so dusty. Just look at my pants.

Henry: Quit worrying about dirt. Just brush it off, Gretchen.

Gretchen: I am, but it's smearing . . . *(Studies Henry's face.)* Ha, ha, so is your face.

Henry: What, am I melting? *(Smears more dirt onto face.)*

Gretchen: *(Giggles.)* Shhhh! She'll hear us. Watch out for that box.

Henry: *(Sits on box, it collapses.)* There, I made a chair.

Gretchen: I want one too. *(Sits on several, but they're full and don't collapse.)*

Henry: You need an empty one.

Gretchen: *(Sits on another.)* Oh well. You know what, Henry? I've decided that the only trouble with Christmas parties is all the work you have to do before them.

Henry: I know. Mom woke me up with the vacuum.

Gretchen: That's what you get for sleeping 'til noon. I got in trouble for my bedroom. It's not like anyone's going in there during the party.

Henry: What about the coats? Mom always makes us pile them up on your bed.

Gretchen: I forgot about that.

Henry: Duh! I got in trouble because my room smells. I just opened the window.

Gretchen: I heard her tell you to get rid of the leftovers; they're what smell.

Henry: That's ridiculous. The containers are all empty.

Gretchen: Yeah, except for the mold growing in them.

Henry: Hey, it's a science project. You can't get in the way of science.

Gretchen: Right, and my closet is an experiment in chaos.

Henry: Is there another way to clean a room? I mean, that's what closets are for, right?

Gretchen: That's my theory. Hey, you don't think there are some presents hidden up here, do you?

Henry: Good thought. Let's look.

Gretchen: Isn't this grandma's lamp? It used to be right by her bed.

Henry: Yeah, I wonder why mom has it up here. Why doesn't grandpa still have it?

Gretchen: Maybe it reminded him too much of grandma.

Henry: Maybe, or maybe it's just too ugly.

Gretchen: Not if it reminds me of grandma, it isn't. I'm going to put this by my bed.

Henry: Figures. Then you can cry yourself to sleep every night, missing her. This will be you . . . *(Bawls like a baby.)* Oh, boo hoo, I miss my grammy.

Gretchen: You miss her too, tough guy.

Henry: Only her cookies. Remember the way she would pick us up and squeeze 'til our eyes popped out? Then she'd slobber all over us making kissy and raspberry noises.

Gretchen: Yeah, like this. *(Blows raspberries on back of hand.)*

Henry: Shhhh! Mom will hear us. Keep looking.

Gretchen: Hey, look, this box is taped shut, the rest are all just folded.

Henry: Looks suspicious. I say we pull it open and check it out.

Gretchen: Mmm, smells good. Careful . . .

Henry: *(Opens box and peers inside.)* Whoa! It's a gingerbread house.

Gretchen: You don't think this is one of grandma's, do you?

Henry: Then it would be five years old!

Gretchen: It still has all the candy stuck on.

Henry: I wonder if it's any good.

Gretchen: I'm not trying it.

Henry: That's 'cuz you're chicken. *(Makes chicken noises.)*

Gretchen: Now who's being noisy? Cut it out. I dare you to try a piece.

Henry: I double dare you.

Gretchen: Fine, we'll both eat one. That way we'll die together.

Henry: I'm trying this gumdrop.

Gretchen: I want this peppermint. Okay, are you ready?

Henry: On the count of three . . . one, two, three. *(Both eat.)*

Gretchen: Mine's fine.

Henry: Mine's like a rock, but it still tastes like cherry. I'll suck on it.

Mom: *(From offstage.)* Henry? Gretchen? Where are you two? *(Pauses.)* Come on you guys, your rooms are still a mess.

Henry: Shhh! Wait.

Mom: I really could use some help.

Gretchen: *(Angrily whispers.)* I did my room already. What does she want from me? I'm not her maid.

Henry: *(Whispers.)* Me neither. I'm eating more of this house.

Mom: *(Still offstage.)* I wonder where they went; maybe they're outside.

Henry: That's right, go look outside and leave us alone. *(Both eat, lights down.)*

Scene 2—The Front Hall

(Henry and Gretchen enter in front of stage, which is dark behind them.)

Gretchen: I don't feel so good.

Henry: My stomach aches.

Gretchen: I think I'm going to throw up.

Henry: I think I'm going to die.

Gretchen: Maybe we shouldn't have eaten that whole wall.

(Enter Mom.)

Mom: There you are, I've been looking all over for you. Did you finish your rooms?

(Kids moan.)

Mom: Oh, come on. I asked you to get started two hours ago. What's going on here?

Henry: My tummy hurts.

Gretchen: Me too.

Mom: *(Feels their foreheads.)* You feel warm. Maybe you're getting the flu.

Henry: But my nose isn't running.

Gretchen: Mine either.

Mom: We can't have a party if you're sick. I'll have to get on the phone and tell everyone not to come.

Henry: No, Mom. We'll get better. Just let us lie down for a while.

Gretchen: I think I'm feeling better already.

Mom: Really?

Gretchen: Yep.

Mom: How miraculous. In that case, it's time you cleaned up your playroom.

Henry: It'll just get messed up again as soon as everyone gets here.

Mom: We can't have people tripping over your toys. They must be put away.

Gretchen: I already picked up all my toys. The rest are Henry's.

Mom: I don't think Henry was playing with your dolls and kitchen set. Work together and it will be done much quicker.

Henry and Gretchen: Okay, Mom.

Mom: You're sure you both feel better?

Henry and Gretchen: Yes, Mom.

Mom: Great. I'll be in the kitchen if you need me. *(Exits.)*

Henry: *(Sarcastic.)* I'm better already, Mom. I already picked up all my toys.

Gretchen: Well, it was worth a try. Come on. *(Lights down.)*

Scene 3—The Dining Room

(Enter Mom, Henry carrying tableware.)

Mom: You two did a nice job on the playroom.

Henry: Thanks, Mom. I did the vacuuming all by myself.

Mom: *(Spreads tablecloth.)* I noticed. The room practically sparkles.

(Henry finishes setting table when Dad and Gretchen enter carrying grocery bags.)

Dad: Hi guys, we're back.

Mom: Wow, that was fast. Did you find everything on the list? *(Looks in bags.)*

Dad: Yep. Gretchen knew where things were.

Mom: Great. If you two will put the groceries away, I'll be finished here in a minute.

Dad: Right. Come on, partner, let's finish the job. *(Exits.)*

Gretchen: I'm right behind you, Dad. *(Exits.)*

Henry: Do we need anything else here, Mom?

Mom: Just the centerpiece, and I had a brilliant idea last night. I can take care of it. If I inspect your room on the way by, will I be happy?

Henry: Mostly . . . okay, I'll go finish. *(Exits.)*

(Enter Dad.)

Dad: What did you say to the kids? I've never seen them so helpful.

Mom: I know. They're excited about the party. They came down with "stomach trouble" earlier, but got miraculously cured when I suggested I'd have to cancel the party.

Dad: Devious, that's what you are. Am I finished with my jobs?

Mom: Yes, unless you want to make the gravy. I just have to go dig out a centerpiece from the attic, then I'll make the salad.

Dad: Gravy is what I do best. *(Exits with Mom.)*

(Enter Henry and Gretchen.)

Gretchen: How's your tummy?

Henry: Miserable.

Gretchen: Do you think we were poisoned?

Henry: I wouldn't be surprised.

Gretchen: What's the trash bag for?

Henry: I'm cleaning out my closet. This is going to be some party tonight.

Gretchen: I just hope we make it through. I keep thinking of all the presents I'll be getting.

Henry: I'd settle for some of that icky pink medicine. My stomach still hurts.

Gretchen: I know.

(Mom screams offstage.)

Gretchen: Mom? What's the matter? *(Runs off stage.)*

Henry: Uh oh.

(Enter Gretchen and Mom, who carries broken gingerbread house. Dad follows, wearing an apron.)

Mom: Henry, do you know anything about this?

Henry: Um . . . no . . . I mean, isn't that one of grandma's?

Mom: Yes, but who ate it? *(Mom and Dad scowl at kids, arms crossed.)*

Henry: You don't think we have mice, do you?

Mom: No, I don't.

Gretchen: If grandma made it, it's pretty old. Maybe it just crumbled all by itself?

Mom: . . . or maybe it didn't.

Henry: Where was it?

Mom: I think you know perfectly well where it was and who ate it. Am I right?

Gretchen: Yes, Mom, that's why our stomachs hurt.

Mom: You just found this today?

Henry: Yes.

Mom: So you were both hiding in the attic when you were supposed to be cleaning up your rooms?

Gretchen: Yes, but we're really sorry. Do you think that old candy will kill us?

Mom: No . . . well, maybe . . . I don't know. We'll just have to see. How are you feeling now?

Gretchen: I'm a little better now.

Henry: I am too, and I'm sorry about the gingerbread house.

Mom: I am very disappointed.

Dad: Me too. Is there any way we can salvage the house?

Gretchen: Can't we just glue some new candy on?

Henry: What about the wall we ate, genius?

Gretchen: Can we build a new one?

Mom: I don't know. I wonder . . . what if I make a nice thick icing?

Henry: Could we use candy pieces like stones and glue them together with icing?

Mom: That would take a long time and I still have plenty to do. All the cleaning is done, but I have to finish dinner. What kind of candy?

Dad: Peanut brittle might work.

Henry: What if Gretchen and I do the gluing?

Gretchen: Yes, Mom, let us do it.

Mom: Who's going to buy the peanut brittle? Your dad just got back from the store.

Henry: We'll walk to the grocery store ourselves.

Mom: All right, you're in charge of the gingerbread house repairs, but I'll make up the icing for you.

Gretchen: Thanks, Mom. We'll do a very good job, you'll see.

Henry: And we'll be very careful crossing the streets to the store, too.

Mom: Great, let's get started. Come on. *(All exit.)*

Scene 4—Later that Night

(Table is cleared, Henry and Gretchen sprawl under the table while playing with toy cars.)

Dad: *(Offstage.)* Thanks for coming. Merry Christmas.

Mom: *(Offstage.)* Good night everybody, Merry Christmas.

(Enter Mom and Dad with coffee cups; sit at table.)

Dad: Well, that was nice. Your roast was perfect this year, dear.

Mom: Thank you. Your gravy was a big hit, too. Did you add a secret ingredient?

Henry: I saw him put sherry in it.

Gretchen: I drank wine tonight?

Dad: The alcohol cooks off, honey, don't worry. You didn't eat much tonight, how's your stomach?

Gretchen: It was still full of old gingerbread house, but it's better.

Mom: You want some of the pink medicine?

Gretchen: No thanks. I'll be fine.

Henry: I think our repair job looked pretty good.

Mom: Mrs. Neal said it looked so good we ought to enter it in the contest at the town hall.

Gretchen: But we only made a part of it, Mom. Wouldn't that be cheating?

Mom: I don't think grandma would mind, if that's what you mean.

Dad: Our house looks great, too.

Gretchen: Do you think Santa was watching us work, Henry? Maybe we'll get extra presents.

Dad: I don't know. He probably already loaded his sack.

Mom: Do you think one night counts that much for Santa?

Henry: If it doesn't, I quit.

Gretchen: Me too.

Dad: Well, if you kids don't get in bed soon, he may have to skip this delivery. You know the rules.

Henry: Do you think he keeps extras, Dad?

Dad: Maybe, but I think you'll never know if you keep stalling.

Gretchen: I'm going. I'm going. *(Slowly moves toward exit.)*

Henry: Last one in bed is a rotten egg. *(Races offstage.)*

Gretchen: Hey . . . *(Races off.)*

Dad: So, what did you ask Santa for Christmas, little girl?

Mom: I think I just got it.

Dad: Ho, ho, ho!

Form 6.1

Script Adaptation Sheet

1. What fairy tale will you adapt?

2. List story elements

3. List revised elements

4. List characters

5. Rename characters

6. Write a summary of the modernized story.

Form 6.1 *Continued*

7. Stage Design: Is a backdrop needed?

8. List furniture required.

9. List actors/costumes needed.

10. List the props.

11. How many stage hands are needed, and what are their jobs?

12. Are stage lights available? Decide what will cue the lights.

13. Are there sound affects? Will they be live or recorded? Cue sounds?

14. Write a description of the opening scene.

7

Story Joke Plays

Story Adaptation

This chapter will explore an entirely different kind of source for stories and plays. Children who have difficulty memorizing math facts often have no trouble remembering song lyrics or story jokes. To encourage these skills, this chapter will give students a new perspective on their favorite story jokes as they inspire new plays. Jokes that are appropriate for students may be difficult to find, but it is possible. The first task is to ask students to write down their favorite story jokes. Give them several days to finish the assignment so that they can ask family and friends for their favorites. Be aware that if you allow children to search the Internet for jokes, they will be exposed to a lot of junk and worse. However, there are two sites listed at the end of this chapter that contain great collections of public domain story jokes. In the classroom, it may be advisable to gather a collection of joke books from the school library and local library for students to search.

Many jokes involve word twists where a word is misunderstood, such as the teacher who complained about her poultry salary. Her friend corrected her and said, "Don't you mean paltry?" The teacher said, "No, I mean poultry, because what I earn is chicken feed." This kind of joke, though funny and a good lesson in the importance of enunciation, is not what you're looking for because there is not enough to work with. Knock-knock jokes are also too short. What can be done with a joke like: "Knock-knock. Who's there? Cargo. Cargo who? Cargo beep, beep, varoom."

A story joke is long, it often involves several characters, and the humor lies in unexpected endings. Many blond jokes are appropriate, as are jokes about, for instance, a priest, a rabbi, and a lawyer. Sure, such jokes use stereotypes, but what a perfect opportunity to discuss tolerance and open minds.

To be safe, screen jokes before continuing with this assignment. Another option is to choose one joke and assign it for the entire class to expand. Decide whether students will work well in small groups or should work independently, and then prepare for surprises, because the results will all be different.

To demonstrate, let's look at one of my favorite blond jokes. It actually involves a blond, a redhead, and a brunette. These three friends were lost in a desert when the blond stubbed her toe. She discovered a bottle buried in the sand, which she picked up and wiped off. Whoosh! Out came a genie who gave them three wishes. The three friends decided to share the wishes. The brunette asked to return safely to her home. Poof! She was gone. The redhead also wanted to go home. Poof! She was gone. The blond said, "Gee, now I'm all by myself. I wish my friends were here." Poof! Poof! There stood her two friends, as the genie returned to his bottle.

To begin, the three friends need names, backgrounds, and personalities. Then, there must be a reason for them to be wandering through a desert, or at least in the sand. If this will be a modern tale, how do we account for the genie? Do we need to modernize him, or must we keep that aspect of the story intact? Finally, the ending must come quickly and unexpectedly to make the joke and humor work.

When I first heard this joke, I imagined three college roommates. Since our young writers are third through eighth graders, our heroines must be younger, so they will become high school freshmen for our new story. Their hair color can symbolize their very different personalities. The brunette is tall and serious, with a strong social conscience. The redhead is petite and slightly plump and she loves children. The blond is a fashionable and bubbly student with artistic talent. While considering appropriate names, more of their personalities emerge. For instance, the brunette becomes Julia. This is a Roman patrician's name, so to honor that, Julia will be interested in architecture. The redhead who loves children is named after the two most famous mothers of all, becoming Marianne. The blond, who is an art and design student, earns the name Tracy.

This is where students will have the biggest opportunity to make their story unique. If this joke is assigned to a class to expand independently, each student will create different characters who might be based on people they know, movie stars, sports figures, or politicians, to name a few. The descriptions of the characters are not just for fun. The information may not become part of the play, but it does help the writer decide how the character speaks and acts, and that is what plays are all about.

Knowing the plot and the character provides pieces of the puzzle, leaving only the setting to be decided. For example, how do the three friends come together in a desert so they can find the genie? Perhaps they are actually on a beach during their spring break. Is there any way to make the same thing happen without a genie? I don't think so, so that will be the beginning of the surprise ending. A perfectly ordinary summer afternoon will become extraordinary. If the audience goes along with the genie, they will wonder what the wishes will be. The first two friends ask for normal things, the blond messes up. Will that be a surprise? Maybe it won't, but how she messes up will be.

Is a wish to go home natural for students on spring break? Hardly. The plot must be adjusted. This is where the writer has to dig through his or her imagination to figure out motivation and solve problems. What if the students are not just on a beach but stranded on an island? Does that solve the problem? Yes it does, because then they would want a quick way home. How are they stranded? What if they take a canoe trip and decide to stop for a picnic lunch on a small island in the middle of the river? Their canoe drifts away, leaving them stranded. Unless the river is very large, they could just swim to shore, so they must be someplace where swimming is not an option. I can think of several such rivers in the United States: parts of the Mississippi, the Yukon, or even the Everglades in Florida. Each river has its own hazards. I'm going to place our students on the Yukon. This scenario no longer needs a spring break, but rather a summer vacation, since the Yukon would still be frozen over in the spring.

Playwriting

Before this story gets any more fantastic, remember middle school children will perform this on a minimal stage. Can that be done? Since the story begins in the canoe, one can be borrowed for the play and placed on a wheeled pallet. If that is not an option, a canoe can be built out of painted cardboard that is also rolled across the stage on a pallet with wheels. When the characters arrive on the beach, they climb out of their canoe. They can roll down an aisle in the theater, pretending that is their river, and then climb up stairs to the stage, if that is how the school auditorium is set up. They can also "row" across the stage in front of a curtain, which opens to reveal the island when they arrive. The curtain provides a touch of mystery but is not really necessary. A rope tied to the front of the canoe can be used by stage hands to pull the canoe back the way it came once the girls climb out, making it "drift" away.

The island can be created in several ways. A backdrop can be painted on canvas, showing the grassy island in the foreground, the river, and a shoreline with pine trees and snowcapped mountains in the distance. Perhaps a painted eagle can help indicate the setting as Alaska. If that is not feasible, a bale of straw can be strewn across the stage to give the effect of windblown grasses. A couple of pine tree cutouts that are lit from the front so that their shadows loom large on the back wall of the stage would help. Sound effects, such as water lapping a shore, the cry of an eagle or ravens, and blowing wind help place the characters in the wilderness.

The next problem is how to create the magic of a genie and his bottle. A trapdoor in the stage floor would be perfect, but if that is unavailable, some extra creativity can also produce a reasonable effect. If curtains are available, they can flutter wildly before the genie appears through them, moving as if an irresistible force is pulling him to the girls. If curtains are unavailable, sound effects like a recording of a tornado or a loud pop like a broken balloon can replace the visual curtain flutter. In that case, the genie can stumble on stage and wipe his clothes as if he just landed on the island and feels disoriented. Whichever way the genie appears, the girls who wish to go home can leave the same way.

As the dialog is created, the need for certain props will become apparent. Don't worry about such details at the beginning, but keep track of them as the story is written.

Finally, should the girls remain stranded after they reappear on the island? Although it may be tempting to have them spend the night, furious with their blond friend, it would be anticlimactic. It is far better to end with a bang than to bore an audience by tying up loose ends and making everyone live happily ever after. The play *Some Luck* is one way this story could unfold.

SOME LUCK

Summary

This play has four scenes and four characters: three girls and a genie. The girls are a blond, a brunette, and a redhead, for reasons which will become clear. The three friends take a canoe trip down the Yukon and stop for lunch on a small island when their luck turns.

Set

Curtains open to reveal a river island.

Props

A canoe is mounted on a wheeled pallet. A thin rope pulls it across the stage. A small cooler, a can of bug spray, and water bottles are in the canoe. A glass bottle with a stopper is needed for Scene 4.

Costumes

The three girls are dressed in long sleeves, long pants, baseball hats, and orange life vests. Jim wears jeans, work boots, a flannel plaid shirt, and a cap with earflaps.

Characters

Julia
Tracy
Marianne
Jim *(genie)*

SOME LUCK

Scene 1—A Day on the Yukon

(Julia sits in the rear, Marianne in the middle, and Tracy in the front of the canoe, which is slowly pulled across the front of the stage. They pretend to paddle with oars.)

Julia: *(Slaps arm, then waves hand as if to ward off flies.)* I can't believe the size of these flies. They're biting, too. Who has the bug spray?

Tracy: *(Rests oar on lap and feels around under seat.)* Hang on, it's under here somewhere. Here you go, Marianne, pass it forward.

Marianne: Here, Julia. You know what your problem is? You taste too good.

Tracy: It's her sweet disposition.

Marianne: It's those blueberry pancakes we had for breakfast.

Julia: Maybe tomorrow we should stick with something stinky. I wonder if flies like the taste of garlic.

Marianne: There's an idea—we could make scrambled eggs with onions and garlic.

Tracy: Stop talking about food, I'm getting hungry.

Julia: Getting hungry? We've been looking for a lunch stop for an hour, ever since your first hunger pains.

Tracy: I don't know what the big deal is. Why can't we just pull up to shore and eat?

Marianne: We keep finding bear tracks in the mud. I don't want to share my sandwiches with bears.

Tracy: Couldn't we just eat here in the canoe?

Julia: Yes, Tracy, but it would be even better to get out and stretch our legs a little.

Marianne: I see an island up ahead. *(Points in front of the canoe.)* Let's take a look and see if it's occupied by any large carnivorous natives.

Julia: I'm game. Let's go take a look.

Tracy: There's so few trees, we should be able to see movement in the grass if there's something on the island. Let's paddle around it before we land.

Marianne: Now you're thinking like a scout. *(The canoe is pulled offstage as the characters continue to row.)*

Julia: Switching. *(Swings oar behind and over head, others also switch.)* Now pull together. One, two . . . pull! *(Lights down.)*

Scene 2—An Island Picnic

(Curtains open to reveal the front of the canoe as the girls walk around, searching the stage floor. The canoe is slowly pulled back offstage during this scene.)

Marianne: I can see where those ducks wandered around, but no bear tracks.

Julia: There aren't even any deer tracks.

Tracy: The grass is pretty wet, but we can use our vests for cushions. *(Tosses vest onto stage and sits.)*

Marianne: This is a great spot. We can see the river in both directions, and the breeze seems to be blowing away the flies. *(Drops vest next to Tracy's and sits.)*

Julia: I'll get the cooler. *(Goes back to the canoe.)* I wish we had a rope to tie up the canoe.

Marianne: There's no trees to tie it to anyway.

Julia: I could stake it.

Tracy: We should start a list of all the things we forgot.

Marianne: Sure, if only we had a piece of paper and a pencil.

Julia: I'll just pull it further onto the beach. *(Rolls it further onstage.)* It will be fine. We're not staying that long anyway. *(Gets cooler.)*

Tracy: Don't forget the cooler.

Julia: I got it, I got it. Oh, do you want your water bottles?

Marianne: Sure, just toss them over.

Julia: Heads up, Tracy. *(Tosses her a bottle.)* Marianne? *(Tosses hers as well, grabs a third, and walks over to picnic site.)*

Marianne: Ah, this is the life. It's hard to believe we were in school just two days ago.

Tracy: I know, and we've been planning this trip for months.

Julia: *(Sits on vest and passes out sandwiches.)* This trip was the only thing that kept me sane during the last week of school. What a great way to start the summer.

Marianne: We should do this every year.

Tracy: Maybe we should try to buy our own canoe so we wouldn't have to borrow my uncle's. Then we could go all summer long, whenever we feel like it.

Julia: Aren't you going to be working at the lodge this summer?

Tracy: Yes, but I'm finished by noon and don't have to be back until dinner time.

Marianne: You have the morning shift—setting up breakfast. I have to wait for everyone to wake up before I can start straightening their rooms. I don't finish until four o'clock.

Julia: That's when my shift at the front desk starts, and it stays busy until I close it at ten.

Tracy: We all get days off, don't we?

Marianne: Not until the last guests go home. I work all summer.

Julia: Me, too, but I don't think we have anyone booked for the next few weeks. We can canoe until then.

Tracy: Have you seen the kitchens yet? It will take me days to clean them out, by the time I sweep out all the cobwebs, wipe the shelves down, and scrub all the dust off the pots and pans.

Marianne: I have to scrub down the rooms, too. Especially the ones that have been empty all winter.

Julia: We had a big crowd during the dog sled races, so things shouldn't be too cobwebby.

Marianne: That's true, and the sheets were washed a long time ago.

Tracy: Then we'll just have to come out as often as we can until the tourists arrive.

Marianne: I can come back out tomorrow.

Julia: I can come out in the morning, then I have to go in to work at the registration desk.

Tracy: Great, let's try to start out earlier tomorrow, like seven o'clock.

Marianne: And miss my chance to sleep in? I need my beauty rest, you know.

Tracy: You're already beautiful enough. Besides, who can sleep in? I'm too used to waking up for school.

Julia: Me, too, and then there's the birds. I heard a woodpecker working on my roof this morning. Talk about a rotten way to wake up . . .

Marianne: There were a couple of ravens outside my window this morning having a loud argument. You should have heard them: clicking their beaks, cawing, whistling . . .

Julia: My grandfather says they have a large vocabulary and are really intelligent.

Marianne: Intelligent or not, they sounded angry. I'll bet a squirrel was bothering their nest or something. It sure is quiet here. Let's lie down a while and take naps before we head back. *(Lies down.)*

Tracy: That sounds great to me. I don't need to rush back to those flies. *(Lies down.)*

Julia: You two are funny—food always seems to make you sleepy. Then again, it is peaceful and quiet here. I guess I could stretch out for a while. *(Lies down.)*

Marianne: Night, night Julia and Tracy.

Tracy: Night, night Marianne and Julia.

Julia: Night, night Marianne and Tracy. *(Lights down as canoe disappears offstage.)*

Scene 3—A Big Deal

(Lights up as the three girls wake up from their naps.)

Julia: Holy cow! How long have we been sleeping?

Marianne: It's four o'clock already—we've been sleeping for hours.

Tracy: Well I feel wonderful so what's the big deal?

Julia: *(Leaps up and looks around frantically.)* There's no big deal except that while we were sleeping, our canoe was stolen.

Marianne: Don't be ridiculous, who would steal our canoe?

Tracy: I thought you pulled it way up on shore. How could it be gone?

Julia: The wind has picked up, the river is rougher, so maybe it was washed away by the waves.

Marianne: Come on, maybe it washed back up down the beach. Let's go look. *(All search the stage in a wide circle, finally disappearing offstage. Reappear on the other side.)*

Julia: We've been around the whole island and there was no sign of it anywhere.

Tracy: My uncle is going to kill me.

Marianne: Not if we never get off this island, he won't.

Julia: Don't be silly. Of course we'll get off the island. Someone will come looking for us if we don't show up for dinner tonight.

Tracy: My mom and dad don't get home 'til dark. They'll never find us out here in the dark.

Julia: My folks went into town and are staying there tonight. They won't notice I'm missing until tomorrow.

Marianne: Well my mom is expecting me to babysit tonight. She'll miss me, don't worry. It's getting a little chilly. Why don't we start a fire, then maybe someone can find us.

Tracy: That's a good idea. I saw some driftwood up the beach that looked dry enough to burn. I'll go get it. *(Exits.)*

Marianne: I'll dig a pit on the beach and look for kindling.

Julia: Do either of you have matches? Mine were in the canoe.

Marianne: There's some in the cooler, in a plastic bag. I'll dig them out.

Julia: Fine. I'll go help Tracy with the driftwood. *(Exits, lights down.)*

Scene 4—Message in a Bottle?

(Julia and Tracy return carrying driftwood and a small bottle.)

Marianne: That didn't take long. Any sign of the canoe?

Tracy: No sign of it, but look what I did find. *(Hands over a glass bottle with a stopper.)*

Marianne: Oooh! Someone's sending messages in bottles. It probably came from a cruise ship. Shall I open it?

Julia: Be my guest.

Tracy: Wait a minute. I found it, I should open it. I mean, what if there's a genie in it or something? It should be *my* three wishes, finders keepers.

Marianne: What if we shared the three wishes—one each. Wouldn't that be better?

Tracy: You're right, I'm sorry. Go ahead, see if you can open it while we stack the fire.

Marianne: As you wish—Man! It's on tight. *(Struggles with stopper, then drops the bottle as it opens with a pop. Stagehand pops balloon offstage.)*

Julia: Well, what's in it?

Marianne: It felt like something was holding the stopper in and then suddenly let go. *(Picks up bottle and peers inside.)* I don't see anything.

Julia: You have such an imagination, Marianne. What could have been holding it in?

Tracy: Maybe it was vacuum-sealed. *(Looks offstage, alarmed.)* Uh, don't look now, you guys, but we're not alone on this island.

Julia: Where did he come from?

Marianne: You don't suppose . . .

(Enter Jim, brushing clothing.)

Jim: *(Yawns and stretches.)* Just when a guy drifts off to sleep . . . *(Looks up and notices girls.)* Hellooo. What have we here? Three pretty girls, an island, and a campfire?

Marianne: *(Stands.)* Don't get any ideas, mister. I'm a black belt in karate. *(Takes up defensive stance.)*

Julia: Me too.

Tracy: I've wrestled bears bigger than you.

Jim: Hey, take it easy ladies. Is this any way to greet your own personal genie?

Julia: Genies don't dress like lumberjacks.

Jim: How would you know? How many have you met?

Marianne: Don't answer that, Julia. Back off, mister, or you'll be on the receiving end of my foot.

Jim: Now listen here, young lady. Nobody, but nobody threatens me, especially not after disturbing my sleep. *(Puffs up chest to look bigger.)* I'm only saying genies dress all different ways. Up north here, we need warm clothes like anyone else.

Julia: If you're a genie, I'm a wombat. How'd you get here anyway?

Jim: Oh, I thought I already explained that. You opened the bottle and out I came.

Tracy: Your pinky wouldn't fit into that bottle, let alone the rest of you.

Jim: Well, you'd be surprised what modern genieologists can do, miss. So, who's going first? Let's get started. The sooner we get this over with, the sooner I can get back to my nap.

Marianne: *(Snorts.)* This I have to see. Okay, I'll play your silly game, mister. What do I have to do, close my eyes and click my heals three times while I repeat the magic words—there's no place like home, there's no place like home . . .

Jim: No, that's for amateurs. Just state your wish and see what happens.

Marianne: Fine. I wish I were off this island and back home.

Jim: That's two wishes. Are you sure?

Marianne: Okay, then I wish I was home. *(Sound of balloon popping offstage. Pauses, then begins to spin in circles until disappearing offstage. Tornado sound effects.)*

Jim: There's one wish. Who's next?

Julia: Ooooh! Me, do me! I wish I was home, too. *(Another pop is heard, she pauses, then spins offstage as well. More tornado sounds.)*

Tracy: Hey! Where'd everybody go? What did you do with them, mister? One minute my friends were standing right next to me, and the next minute they were gone. Where are they?

Jim: Home, of course. You like that tornado effect? I thought of that myself. It's so much more fun to watch than a puff of smoke.

Tracy: Yes. I mean, no. I don't want to get caught in any tornado. What kind of game is this anyway? No one can do that. Are you some kind of magician? Where are the mirrors?

Jim: Call it whatever you want, it makes no difference to me, and no, there are no mirrors. Now, what is your wish?

Tracy: Oh man, I don't know. I can't believe I'm standing on some stupid little island in the middle of the Yukon with some lunatic who thinks he's a genie. Where are my friends when I need them? I hate this. I wish they were still here . . . *(Gasps as a pop sounds offstage, then both Julia and Marianne spin back onstage and fall by the driftwood. Jim spins offstage.)*

Tracy: Wait! Where are you going? Uh, oh.

Julia: Oh, no!

Marianne: Tracy . . . ?

(Tracy covers her mouth in surprise and shrugs her shoulders. Lights down.)

Story Joke Plays   97

Sources for Story Jokes

The following Web sites contain clean story jokes.

http://www.opotiki2.co.nz/downloads/jokes/jokes1.htm.

http://www.jokeuniversity.com.

Extensions

To produce this play, there are several jobs for students who will not be actors.

1. Build a canoe on wheels

   - Begin with two borrowed wagons and tie them together. Or build a wheeled platform.
   - Cut a discarded refrigerator box into a long, narrow rectangle for the side of the canoe and attach it to one side of the wagons. Paint the cardboard red.
   - Attach a thin rope or wire that will reach across the length of the stage to the front wagon's handle or the platform.
   - Build or borrow three oars.

2. Create the island

   - Paint a backdrop with a river rising three feet above the floor, a sandy shoreline topped with evergreen trees, and snowcapped mountains in the distance. An eagle perching in a tree and another swooping through the sky help place the action in Alaska.
   - Obtain a bale of hay and spread it across the floor of the stage in front of the backdrop.

3. Record a soundtrack

   - Find or make recordings of rushing water, splashing (oars entering the water), eagle cries, raven clicks and caws, wolf howls, bear growls, duck quacks, a tornado, strong wind, and the sounds of popping balloons. Cue the sounds to the play.

8

Poetry Plays

This chapter presents a way for students to explore poetry as a story. As in Chapter 1, we will use poems as springboards for creative writing exercises. These will be turned into plays instead of choral readings or readers theatre.

The most powerful poems make a person feel something, but that doesn't mean they are strictly about feelings. Some describe situations about which a person feels strongly, such as the loss of a family pet. Some are about characters who must make decisions, much like stories. They can also be about someone funny or a funny way of looking at ordinary things, the way Shel Silverstein's poems do.

Whenever a class reads poetry, this chapter can enhance the experience. Students should be familiar with the mechanics of poetry: metaphor, simile, assonance, meter, rhyme, etc. Once they begin to study different poets, why not have them compare the poems to stories? For instance, one difference between poetry and stories is the way poems describe a brief, intense moment or situation, while stories offer background information and a fuller picture. That is not to say that poetry is incomplete or needs embellishment, but rather that poems present a moment of significance, which creative writers can use as the basis for a story.

Story Adaptation

One of my favorite poems is reprinted below and will be the basis for one script created in this chapter. Take a moment to enjoy Robert Frost's "The Road Not Taken."

The Road Not Taken

Robert Frost (1874–1963)

1 Two roads diverged in a yellow wood,
2 And sorry I could not travel both
3 And be one traveler, long I stood
4 And looked down one as far as I could
5 To where it bent in the undergrowth;

6 Then took the other, as just as fair,
7 And having perhaps the better claim,
8 Because it was grassy and wanted wear;
9 Though as for that the passing there
10 Had worn them really about the same,

11 And both that morning equally lay
12 In leaves no step had trodden black.
13 Oh, I kept the first for another day!

14   Yet knowing how way leads on to way,
15   I doubted if I should ever come back.
16   I shall be telling this with a sigh
17   Somewhere ages and ages hence:
18   Two roads diverged in a wood, and I—
19   I took the one less traveled by,
20   And that has made all the difference.

This poem is a nostalgic look at a decision and its effect on the life of the poet. There are no consequences described, yet the intersection of two roads or paths is used as a metaphor for a significant choice. The reader must imagine the scene and figure out why taking "the one less traveled by" has "made all the difference" in the end. There are clues about the time of the year, it is "a yellow wood," which could mean the journey was taken in the autumn—a metaphor for the later years in life. Many images have double meanings.

Because there are so few specifics in this poem, there are lots of decisions that must be made. Clustering will help plan the story, whether this is a project for the class to work on in teams or as a large group. The questionnaire at the end of this chapter will steer the clustering decisions. Once the story in outlined in the questionnaire, the original story can be converted into a script.

Playwriting

What choice is described in Robert Frost's poem? Is it a man choosing between two women, a student choosing whether or not to cheat, or a teenager choosing between two career paths? There are many other possibilities, but for this exercise, let's say it is a teenager who must choose between two girlfriends, the time is now, and their names are Christine and Alicia. The teenager's name is Ben.

Taking a cue from the poem, the teen has to choose because he knows he cannot date both girls. He imagines life with Alicia far into the future, when "it bent in the undergrowth" or she (and he) grow old. He chooses Christine, who is "just as fair." How can lines 7 and 8, "And having perhaps the better claim, Because it was grassy and wanted wear," be interpreted in this scenario? Perhaps Christine has the advantage because she is prettier (grassy) and less popular (wanted wear). In retrospect, Ben decides in lines 9 and 10 that they were very similar. Both "that morning" were unattached (had no other boyfriends), yet one is set aside "for another day!" Does he expect Alicia to wait for him? No, because even then Ben knew that once he chose Christine, he could never go back to that same place and change his mind for Alicia. The sigh shows he is nostalgic for that time and place. Does Robert Frost tell us whether his traveler is happy with the choice? No, he says only that it "has made all the difference." Wouldn't it be wonderful to allow our audience members to decide for themselves as well? We'll set the tone with the title *All the Difference*.

ALL THE DIFFERENCE

Summary

A teenager named Ben must choose between Alicia and Christine. How does he make that decision when he loves both? Years later, how does he feel?

Set

Scene 1: a backyard with a few pieces of lawn furniture. Scene 2: a cafeteria where a couple of cafeteria tables replace the lawn furniture. An industrial-sized trash can with liner sits on the side.

Props

Two baseball mitts, a baseball. Cafeteria trays, paper sack with a lunch, small milk carton.

Costumes

Present-day casual—jeans, sweaters.

Characters

Ben
Jerry
Alicia
Christine

ALL THE DIFFERENCE

Scene 1—The Backyard

(Lights up as Ben and Jerry enter with mitts and a baseball. They toss it back and forth.)

Ben: Sure, I want to go to homecoming, but not alone. That's pretty lame, isn't it?

Jerry: I guess so. Just ask someone. It's no big deal. It's not like you're asking them to marry you or anything.

Ben: Yeah, but I can't decide between Alicia or Christine. Plus, they're friends, so if I ask one, the other will know. I have to practice grounders, so give me some.

Jerry: Poor baby, having to choose between those two. Neither one would even look at me.

Ben: Nora looked and you're taking her, aren't you?

Jerry: Yeah, but she gets so jealous. Now I have to figure out how to get her to back off.

Ben: Didn't she toss an entire roll of toilet paper into your front trees when she thought you liked, who was it, Marci?

Jerry: Yeah, right, like, who's Marci anyway?

Ben: How should I know? Probably one of her friends. Give me a fast ball.

Jerry: Fast ball, eh? You asked for it. . . . I wish you'd seen Nora when I caught her in my front yard. The look on her face . . . she did this disco step and tossed the roll as she went. It was so funny, man; I thought I'd bust a gut.

Ben: *(Shakes mitt hand like it stings.)* Where were your folks?

Jerry: At a movie. She went home before they got back.

Ben: You had to clean it up?

Jerry: Yeah, but it was worth it. *(Winds up like a pitcher.)*

Ben: I like girls with a sense of humor.

Jerry: Yeah, we laughed ourselves silly.

Ben: I wish I had your guts when it comes to talking to girls.

Jerry: Hey, it's no big deal. What, are you scared?

Ben: I'm petrified they'll think I'm stupid the minute I open my mouth.

Jerry: So they laugh at you. Who cares? *(Pensively tosses ball into own mitt.)* We're not in second grade, besides they're just as scared as we are.

Ben: Yeah, but they'll gossip with their friends, and then *everyone* will know how stupid I am.

Jerry: Listen, they're just girls, flesh and blood like you and me.

Ben: . . . and long hair and lip gloss and perfume. They're so different; they're like aliens. Besides, they talk so much—no secret is safe.

Jerry: So, don't tell them any secrets.

Ben: What if they think I'm boring? What do you talk to girls about, not sports—they hate sports stats and couldn't care less about the players.

Jerry: Some do. Remember Maureen? She keeps the stats for her soccer team, she's very good at it, doesn't miss a thing.

Ben: Yeah, but she's different; she's athletic.

Jerry: So, talk to an athlete, or you talk to someone in class, find a study partner.

Ben: That's not a bad idea. We'd have something to talk about, class, and something to do, study. It would be good practice, even if I'm not crazy about her.

Jerry: Sure, and then who knows? One minute you'll be reading Emily Dickinson and the next you'll be gazing into each other's eyes . . .

Ben: . . . and I'll notice they're crossed behind her thick glasses . . .

Jerry: . . . and she has bad breath . . .

Ben: . . . and I'll fall madly in love . . .

Jerry: . . . and she'll break your heart when she moves away to college.

Ben: Oh, so I'll be studying with a brainy one, eh?

Jerry: Of course. You did say study, right? You want a girl who knows what she's doing.

Ben: What if I pick a girl who needs help?

Jerry: She'd have to come to you for help because she notices you're acing things.

Ben: That blows it for me. My grades are in the toilet.

Jerry: So you're back with the smart girl.

Ben: Okay, fine, so what do I say? Excuse me, I couldn't help noticing that you're smart and I'm not, so maybe we could study together? What's in it for her? Who would ever agree to that?

Jerry: Someone who already likes you? Besides, that's not a bad line. You started with flattery and moved on to self-deprecation.

Ben: Okay, now that just doesn't sound right.

Jerry: It means you put yourself down, show some humility. Girls go for that.

Ben: Great, now I'm back to a girl who tells her friends she helps the stupid guy. I'm doomed.

(Enter Alicia and Christine.)

Alicia: Hi Ben. Can we play?

Ben: You got a mitt?

Christine: I brought one.

Jerry: Here, Alicia. You use mine, I don't need it.

Alicia: Thank you, Jerry. You're sweet.

Jerry: No, it's nothing. It doesn't fit me anymore anyway.

Alicia: Is this how I wear it?

Jerry: Here, let me help. *(Stands behind her and adjusts the mitt, smells her hair.)*

Christine: *(Aside to Ben.)* Those two could be a while, Ben. Come on, toss it to me.

Ben: Here it comes.

Christine: Hey, do you know if Jerry has a date for homecoming yet?

Ben: Probably with Nora, why?

Christine: Really? I heard they broke up. I mean . . . oh, rats! I shouldn't have said that. Do you think he heard?

Ben: No, he's oblivious. Who told you?

Christine: Nora was complaining in gym class today, acting like they were ancient history.

Ben: She hasn't told Jerry yet.

Christine: Are you gonna tell him?

Ben: I probably should—give him a chance to run for his life when he sees her coming, you know, prepare himself for the worst.

Christine: I think he'll be better off without her. She's horribly jealous and controlling. Look how he's getting along with Alicia.

Ben: Yeah, he'll bounce like silly putty.

Christine: Alicia may catch him on the rebound then.

Ben: Let's see if she can catch. Hey you two, you gonna play or not?

Jerry: What? No, I mean yeah, throw the ball. I'm ready.

Ben: I hope so, man. Heads up. *(Tosses ball. Jerry runs off stage as if to catch it. Lights down.)*

Scene 2—The Cafeteria

(A couple of cafeteria tables replace the lawn furniture. An industrial-sized trash can with liner sits on the side. Ben sits with a tray of food, facing the audience. Lights up as Jerry enters with a paper lunch bag and milk carton.)

Jerry: Sorry I'm late. I had to talk to old man Stone.

Ben: I thought maybe you left or something. You in trouble with Stone?

Jerry: No, I'm his aide, remember? I had to tell him about the field trip tomorrow.

Ben: You're kidding, it's tomorrow?

Jerry: You forgot the field trip to the stadium? How could you forget? We've been talking about it for weeks.

Ben: Yeah, but I thought it was later, that's all.

Jerry: Don't forget to bring your mitt so you can get Johnson to sign it.

Ben: Right, I just have to find it. Haven't seen it for a while.

Jerry: What's the matter with you, you can't remember anything? Oh, I get it, there's a girl, isn't there?

Ben: No, there's no girl. How can I see a girl when I'm grounded for life?

Jerry: So when will that change?

Ben: When do report cards go out?

Jerry: Ah, my friend, the end is in sight. They get mailed next week—arrive home within days. Depends on whether they have good news or bad. The good news moves slowly, the bad news goes fast. At least that's been my experience.

Ben: Well, hard times will end by break, then. I think I've brought everything up, thanks to Christine.

Jerry: I knew it. There is a girl. So, spill it . . .

Ben: What? We're not dating or anything. I did ask her to study history with me, though.

Jerry: Ha, good man. You took my advice.

Ben: I guess so, except she came to me. I didn't have to say anything stupid except "okay."

Jerry: Well, great. That wasn't so hard, was it?

Ben: No. How's Nora?

Jerry: Nora who?

Ben: You know, have you . . .

Jerry: No, so far I've managed to avoid her. She's always surrounded by a gaggle of girls and she's really good at pretending she doesn't see me.

Ben: What about walking home?

Jerry: She stays after to watch the basketball team practice. I think she wants to be a cheerleader or something.

Ben: She has the lungs for it.

Jerry: You got that right. Speaking of lungs, I want to sit with Alicia on the bus ride. I figure it's a good time to talk.

Ben: No problem. I'll sit with Christine; we can keep studying.

Jerry: Hey, you've been on field trips before. No one studies on the bus, man. It is prime time for being with your girl. I mean, you're at school, but not. Everyone's talking, and you have a captive audience if you plan the seating right.

Ben: Maybe for you. You don't get all tongue-tied. I always sit in the middle with a book.

Jerry: So, sit with Christine; just don't study. Maybe act like you want to, but . . . ask about her, what's her favorite CD, has she been to the stadium before, how many kids in her family . . . that kind of stuff.

Ben: I already know all that. We talk when I walk her home.

Jerry: Man, you're way ahead of me then. Alicia is so shy that I only get two words out of her per question. She's like "yes," "no," "sometimes," or "I don't know."

Ben: Maybe she's afraid of Nora.

Jerry: Nah, she knows Nora's friends and steers clear. She thinks they're snobs.

Ben: She's right.

Jerry: I know. I can't believe I didn't see it before.

Ben: So, it's you and Alicia these days?

Jerry: Yeah, I guess so. She's quiet and smart, she likes to read, and did you know she's in band?

Ben: What does she play?

Jerry: She's on the French horn. I never noticed her before because I couldn't see her past the tubas and trombones.

Ben: Before what?

Jerry: Before we played catch that day.

Ben: Was that the first time you two talked?

Jerry: Yeah, I think it was.

Ben: That's the first time I talked to Christine, too. I remember we were talking about girls, and next thing—they showed up.

Jerry: That was weird, wasn't it?

Ben: It reminds me of a famous poem I read once. Something about two roads in a woods and the choice made all the difference. So, what if I'd given Alicia my mitt instead of you? Things would be different, now, right?

(Enter Alicia and Christine, carrying lunch trays.)

Christine: Hi Ben. Are these seats taken?

Ben: They are now. Help yourselves.

Jerry: *(Stands.)* Let me take your tray. You forgot a napkin. Here, I have extras.

Alicia: Thanks, Jerry.

Christine: I like the service in this restaurant.

Ben: We serve only the finest cardboard burgers and sandpaper napkins. Never cloth, oh, no!

Christine: *(Giggles.)* At least the price is right.

Jerry: . . . Especially when you pack your own. Which reminds me, Alicia, mom made her brownies again. Want one?

Alicia: Yes, thank you, Jerry.

(Ben and Jerry exchange glances, lights down.)

Story Adaptation

Here is another powerful poem to adapt, Edgar Allan Poe's "The Raven." The main character is upset by the loss of his beloved Lenore. His emotional distress increases when a raven arrives and perches over a doorway. There is irony in this poem as well as a great deal of symbolism.

Before deciding how to adapt "The Raven" into a script, review the text below. Listen for the sounds of the meter, the pace, the alliteration. Watch for scene changes or descriptions and decide how many characters are involved in the action.

The Raven

Edgar Allan Poe (1809–1849)

Once upon a midnight dreary, while I pondered, weak and weary,
Over many a quaint and curious volume of forgotten lore—
While I nodded, nearly napping, suddenly there came tapping,
As of some one gently rapping, rapping at my chamber door.
"'Tis some visitor," I muttered, "tapping at my chamber door—
Only this and nothing more.

Ah, distinctly I remember it was in the bleak December;
And each separate dying ember wrought its ghost upon the floor.
Eagerly I wished the morrow;—vainly I had sought to borrow
From my books surcease of sorrow—sorrow for the lost Lenore—
For the rare and radiant maiden whom the angels name Lenore—
Nameless *here* for evermore.

And the silken, sad, uncertain rustling of each purple curtain
Thrilled me—filled me with fantastic terrors never felt before;
So that now, to still the beating of my heart, I stood repeating
"'Tis some visitor entreating entrance at my chamber door—
Some late visitor entreating entrance at my chamber door;—
This it is and nothing more."

Presently my soul grew stronger; hesitating then no longer,
"Sir," said I, "or Madam, truly your forgiveness I implore;
But the fact is I was napping, and so gently you came rapping,
And so faintly you came tapping, tapping at my chamber door,
That I scarce was sure I heard you"—here I opened wide the door;—
Darkness there and nothing more.

Deep into that darkness peering, long I stood there wondering, fearing,
Doubting, dreaming dreams no mortal ever dared to dream before;
But the silence was unbroken, and the stillness gave no token,
And the only word there spoken was the whispered word, "Lenore!"
This I whispered, and an echo murmured back the word "Lenore!"
Merely this and nothing more.

Back into the chamber turning, all my soul within me burning,
Soon again I heard a tapping somewhat louder than before.
"Surely," said I, "surely that is something at my window lattice;

Let me see, then, what thereat is, and this mystery explore—
Let my heart be still a moment and this mystery explore—
'Tis the wind and nothing more!"

Open here I flung the shutter, when, with many a flirt and flutter
In there stepped a stately Raven of the saintly days of your.
Not the least obeisance made he; not a minute stopped or stayed he;
But, with mien of lord or lady, perched above my chamber door—
Perched upon a bust of Pallas just above my chamber door—
Perched, and sat, and nothing more.

Then this ebony bird beguiling my sad fancy into smiling,
By the grave and stern decorum of the countenance it wore,
"Though thy crest be shorn and shaven, thou," I said, "art sure no craven,
Ghastly grim and ancient Raven wandering from the Nightly shore—
Tell me what thy lordly name is on the Night's Plutonian shore!"
Quoth the Raven, "Nevermore."

Much I marveled this ungainly fowl to hear discourse so plainly,
Though its answer little meaning—little relevance bore;
Fore we cannot help agreeing that no living human being
Ever yet was blessed with seeing bird above his chamber door—
Bird or beast upon the sculptured bust above his chamber door,
With such name as "Nevermore."

But the Raven, sitting lonely on the placid bust, spoke only
That one word, as if his soul in that one word he did outpour.
Nothing farther then he uttered—not a feather then he fluttered—
Till I scarcely more than muttered "Other friends have flown before—
On the morrow *he* will leave me, as my hopes have flown before."
Then the bird said "Nevermore."

Startled at the stillness broken by reply so aptly spoken,
"Doubtless," said I, "what it utters is its only stock and store
Caught from some unhappy master whom unmerciful Disaster
Followed fast and followed faster till his songs one burden bore—
Till the dirges of his Hope that melancholy burden bore
Of 'Never—nevermore.' "

But the Raven still beguiling all my fancy into smiling,
Straight I wheeled a cushioned seat in front of bird, and bust and door;
Then, upon the velvet sinking, I betook myself to linking
Fancy unto fancy, thinking what this ominous bird of yore—
What this grim, ungainly, ghastly, gaunt, and ominous bird of yore
Meant in croaking "Nevermore.":

This I sat engaged in guessing, but no syllable expressing
To the fowl whose fiery eyes now burned into my bosom's core;
This and more I sat divining, with my head at ease reclining
On the cushion's velvet lining that the lamplight gloated o'er,
But whose velvet violet lining with the lamplight gloating o'er,
She shall press, ah, nevermore!

Then, methought, the air grew denser, perfumed from an unseen censer
Swung by Seraphim whose foot-falls tinkled on the tufted floor.
"Wretch," I cried, "thy God hath lent thee—ty these angels he hath sent thee
Respite—respite and nepenthe from thy memories of Lenore;
Quaff, oh quaff this kind nepenthe and forget this lost Lenore!"
Quoth the Raven "Nevermore."

"Prophet!" said I, "thing of evil! Prophet still, if bird or devil!—
Whether Tempter sent, or whether tempest tossed thee here ashore,
Desolate yet all undaunted, on this desert land enchanted—
On this home by Horror haunted—tell me truly, I implore—
Is there—*is* there balm in Gilead?—tell me—tell me, I implore!"
Quoth the Raven "Nevermore."

"Prophet!" said I, "thing of evil!—prophet still, if bird or devil!
By that Heaven that bends above us—by that God we both adore—
Tell this soul with sorrow laden if, within the distant, Aidenn,
It shall clasp a sainted maiden whom the angels name Lenore—
Clasp a rare and radiant maiden whom the angels name Lenore."
Quoth the Raven "Nevermore."

"Be that word our sign of parting, bird or fiend!" I shrieked, upstarting—
"Get thee back into the tempest and the Night's Plutonian shore!
Leave no black plume as a token of that lie thy soul hath spoken!
Leave my loneliness unbroken!—quit the bust above my door!
Take thy beak from out my heart, and take thy form from off my door!"
Quoth the Raven "Nevermore."

And the Raven, never flitting, still is sitting, *still* is sitting
On the pallid bust of Pallas just above my chamber door;
And his eyes have all the seeming of a demon's that is dreaming,
And the lamp-light o'er him streaming throws his shadow on the floor;
Any my soul from out that shadow that lies floating on the floor
Shall be lifted—nevermore!

This poem is almost the exact opposite of the Frost poem because it is so full of details and is very specific. There is definite rhyme and meter that set the pace, just like the poems from Chapter 1. However, there is no need to create a character, setting, or time frame because that has all been clearly set out by Mr. Poe. The challenge in creating a script from this poem is to retain the pace and sense of dread that builds from the first stanza and doesn't end until the main character collapses on the floor in the last stanza.

Playwriting

Because this poem is written in first person, it would be possible to create a monologue. Luckily the raven speaks, so we can instead write this script as a dialog. It may be interesting to add a narrator, but that can be decided once the characters begin to speak.

The next step is to decide whether the main character is talking with someone. Because this is about a man's anguish, the main character should be a sympathetic male or female, such as a close friend or relative. Another option is to create a monolog, where the character addresses the audience.

In that case, it is not necessary to name him. In order to allow more students to participate in this play, there is another intriguing option. What if several students take the stage to recite the lines of the main character? The actors change as the character's emotions change from gloomy to happy to gloomy to angry. In that case, the main character(s) must be named, perhaps Edgar.

Because one of the most memorable parts of this poem is the rhythm, careful attention must be paid to the lines given to Edgar. Mr. Poe builds suspense and horror through his careful pacing. His character becomes fearful and then tries to calm himself with less and less success. In addition, there is liberal use of assonance and rhyme. To honor that, lines in the play must be structured to allow these sounds to emerge and work their magic.

A seventh- or eighth-grade audience can understand Poe's subject matter but probably does not have the means to build an elaborate set. A backdrop painted to look like bookshelves on either side of a window through which a stormy night is shown is a great assignment for an art class. Otherwise, one tall bookcase filled with books can work just as well. Dim lights that flash at the proper moment can portray a stormy night. Other classmates can work on creating a sound recording of rain, thunder, and blowing wind.

In this play, the main part of Edgar is split into six different ones, each representing a different mood. The raven also has a speaking part. This can be staged as a readers theatre piece, with all the characters arranged on the stage in the beginning. Edgars one-through-six enter together and make a small speech to explain their presence. They take their chairs arranged across the center of the stage. The raven remains out of sight until Scene 2. See *Once Upon a Midnight Dreary.*

ONCE UPON A MIDNIGHT DREARY

Summary

Edgar sits in his study on a gloomy night. A mysterious visitor arrives. Several actors portray the different moods of Edgar as he speaks with his visitor.

Set

A backdrop painted to look like bookshelves gives the impression of a gentleman's private library. Include on the backdrop a window showing a stormy night. Six chairs are arranged on each side of the backdrop, angled toward the audience. A tall stool for the raven is placed right or left downstage, opposite to the side from which the raven will enter.

Props

A small velvet pillow.

Costumes

The raven wears all black, black hair or a black hood, and a black tailcoat. All of the actors playing Edgar wear similar clothes, yet each has some detail that hints at their mood. Edgar #1 is disheveled from waking, Edgar #2 is frightened, Edgar #3 is determined, Edgar #4 is happy and excited, Edgar #5 is tense and depressed, and Edgar #6 is angry.

Characters

Edgars #1 through 6
The Raven

ONCE UPON A MIDNIGHT DREARY

(All Edgars enter and sit in chairs, assuming postures that fit their emotions. Edgar #1 stands and walks to center stage.)

Edgar #1: We are Edgar. We each represent different moods of the same man. *(Steps to side.)*

Raven: *(Enters.)* I am . . . Raven. *(Flips tails haughtily, then exits.)*

Edgar #1: *(To audience, yawns as though waking.)* What a cold and dreary midnight. I am truly weak and weary. No more pondering quaint and curious volumes of forgotten lore. I must have nodded off, nearly napping. Listen there. I hear a tapping, sudden rapping, rapping at my chamber door. What is it? 'Tis a visitor, only this, and nothing more.

But who's about on such a bleak December night, when each separate fire's embers wring their ghosts upon the floor. Will it never be tomorrow? There's no comfort from my sorrow, in this reading of these ancient books of yore. Still I miss my sweet Lenore, my beautiful amore, a rare and radiant maiden whom the angels name Lenore. Nameless *here* for evermore. *(Sighs deeply and returns to chair.)*

Edgar #2: *(Slowly walks to center. Acts frightened. Speaks quickly.)* Ah Lenore . . . I listen to the silken, sad, uncertain rustling of those purple curtains. They thrill me while they fill me with a terror like I never felt before. Is she there? No, I'll still my heart's loud beating, with this standing and repeating, 'Tis some caller, some late visitor seeking entrance to my chamber. It is this, only this, and nothing more.

Listen as my soul grows stronger; then I hesitate no longer. *(Walks toward the audience.)* Sir or Madam, your forgiveness I implore. I was napping and so faintly, yes, so gently you came rapping, that I wasn't sure I heard you tapping at my chamber door. *(Peers into audience. Cowers.)*

It's dark there, nothing more. Yet I wonder, no, I fear, my eyes see nothing while there actually is something. The silence is unbroken and the stillness gives no token. Was I dreaming; am I dreaming? What's that whisper?

Raven: *(Offstage.)* Lenore!

Edgar #2: *(Whispers.)* Lenore? Is there an echo?

Raven: *(Offstage.)* Lenore!

Edgar #2: 'Tis an echo, merely this and nothing more. *(Returns to chair.)*

May be copied for classroom use. *Literary Ideas and Scripts for Young Playwrights* by Lisa Kaniut Cobb (Portsmouth, NH: Teacher Ideas Press) © 2004.

Edgar #3: *(Clasps hands behind back and paces with determination.)* Now I'll go back to my study even though my soul is burning. *(Stops.)* There it is. There's that tapping, only louder than before. Surely, yes, oh surely something's knocking at my lattice. Let me see then, I must look and thus this mystery explore. It's the wind outside my window. 'Tis the wind and nothing more.

(Walks resolutely toward window.) I must look now. What is out there? I must solve this mystery. I must stop my heart from pounding, sounding out its loud alarm, just one moment while this mystery I explore. Surely 'tis the wind. Merely this and nothing more. *(Returns to chair. Sound of slamming door, wind offstage.)*

Raven: *(Enters shaking jacket like it is wings that are wet. Walks regally to stool, turns, flips tails out and sits, watching Edgars.)*

Edgar #4: *(Walks forward excitedly.)* I opened wide the shutter, and in with flirt and flutter, there stepped a stately Raven from the saintly days of yore. With no sign of "by your leave," nor one moment's hesitation, but with look of lord or lady came he in. He fluttered to that perch there, right beside my chamber door. Now he's perching there and sitting, nothing more. *(Addresses Raven.)* Your ebony face beguiles and I cannot help my smiles. My, you wear the grave and sternest countenance. Though your head is shorn and shaven you are certainly no craven, ghastly, grim and ancient Raven, wand'ring from the nightly shore. Tell me what your lordly name is on this night's Plutonian shore?

Raven: Nevermore.

Edgar #4: *(Amazed.)* How might *you*, ungainly fowl, ever learn to speak so plainly? *(Shakes head, no longer impressed.)* It means nothing, it's not relevant, I'm sure. Though not everyone is blessed by seeing bird, or any being, perched so still and smart beside their chamber door. Yet you sit there perched and named by—Nevermore? *(Studies the bird then shrugs and returns to chair.)*

Edgar #5: *(Stands, rolling head and shoulders as though stiff and bored.)* There you sit all sad and lonely and you'll speak that one word only? It's as if with that one word you did your Raven soul outpour. Nothing further will you utter? Not one feather will you flutter? Will you merely sit and mutter that one word beside my door? Other friends have flown before. On the morrow you'll quit my door, and you'll leave just as my hopes have done before.

Raven: Nevermore.

Edgar #5: *(Huge accepting sigh. Speaks mournfully to audience.)* Doubtless though the stillness broken, by one word so aptly spoken, reveals this bird's entire stock and store. Taught by one unhappy master whom unmerciful disaster, followed fast and followed faster by even more disasters left him with one lonely song, one burden more. He repeats it like a dirge, dashing hopes of lord and master and he'll learn no other word but "nevermore." *(Sits, shaking head.)*

Raven: Nevermore.

Edgar #4: *(Rises, smiles, and sits on floor center stage, near Raven.)* Still, Dear Raven, you're beguiling and I cannot help my smiling. Shall I sit and rest a while as you have done? Will you also steer my thinking, while my fancy's linking fancy, wondering what you mean by this one ominous word? You grim, ungainly, ghastly, gaunt and ominous bird, what meaning lies in croaking "Nevermore?"

Raven: Nevermore.

Edgar #4: *(Studies Raven for several beats, then stands, shrugs, and returns to chair, leaving pillow on the floor.)*

Edgar #2: *(Rises, picks up pillow, paces with it. Speaks quickly, frightened.)* Shall I sit engaged in guessing, but no syllable expressing, while those fowl and fiery eyes burn into my bosom's core? This and more I'll sit divining, with my head at ease reclining on this cushion's velvet lining that the lamplight gloated o'er. *(Looks at pillow with disgust.)* Ah, this velvet, violet lining with the lamplight gloating o'er, *she* shall press, no, nevermore. *(Drops pillow and rushes back to seat.)*

Raven: Nevermore.

Edgar #5: *(Sits forlornly center stage on pillow and faces Raven.)* Methinks the air grows denser, perfumed by an unseen censor, swung by Seraphim whose footfalls tinkle near. *(Addresses Raven.)* Wretch! Thy God hath lent thee, by those angels he hath sent thee. Bring respite, respite and nepenthe from my thoughts of lost Lenore. *(Sniffs the air.)* Quaff, oh quaff this soothing nepenthe, and forget my lost Lenore.

Raven: Nevermore.

(Edgar #5 returns to chair.)

Edgar #3: *(Stands and uses hands as scales to weigh these thoughts.)* Prophet. Thing of evil, yet a prophet *still* if bird or devil, whether Tempter sent or whether tempest tossed. Des'late yet all undaunted, in this desert land enchanted, in this home by horror haunted, tell me truly, I implore. *Is* there . . . *is* there balm in Gilead? Tell me, tell me I implore.

Raven: Nevermore.

(Edgar #3 sighs heavily, tosses hands in desperation, and returns to seat.)

Edgar #6: *(Storms toward Raven, angry.)* Prophet! Thing of evil! Bird or devil? I don't care. By the heaven bending o'er us, by the God we both adore, tell this soul with sorrow laden . . . if within the distant Aidenn, it shall clasp a sainted maiden whom the angels name Lenore. Will I clasp that radiant maiden whom the angels name Lenore? Will I see her, can I hold her whom the angels name Lenore?

Raven: Nevermore.

Edgar #6: Be that word your final good-bye, bird or fiend it's time you *did* fly! Go on, back into the tempest, and the night's Plutonian shore. *(Waves arms at bird to shoo it away.)* Leave no black plume as a token of that lie that you have spoken. Leave my loneliness unbroken. Quit your place beside my door. Take your beak from out my heart and your carcass out my door. Get you gone, you rascal Raven. Get you gone!

Raven: Nevermore.

(Edgar #6 gasps and then swoons to the floor.)

Raven: *(Remains still for several counts, then turns to the audience with an evil grin.)* And still I'm sitting, never flitting, always sitting on this stool, sitting on this stool inside this wretched room's décor. Though my eyes have all the seeming of a demon's that is dreaming, and the lamp-light that is streaming throws my shadow on the floor, I'll wait here for that soul in a heap upon the floor. That lonely shadow that is floating shall be lifted. . . . Nevermore. *(Lights down.)*

Form 8.1

Questionnaire for Clustering a Poem to a Play

1. What poem will you adapt?

2. What is the central theme of the poem?

3. Who are the characters in the moment?

4. What is the historical period?

5. Name the characters.

Form 8.1 *Continued*

6. **Write a paragraph to summarize the conflict or change that takes place.**

7. **What costumes are needed?**

8. **List the props.**

9. **Are stage lights available? Decide what will cue the lights.**

10. **Will there be sounds or music, and what will be their cue?**

9

Historical Plays

Story Adaptation

Many students in fourth to eighth grade enjoy historical fiction; ask any children's librarian. The Pleasant Company dolls and their books, for example, are based on fictional characters that portray life during certain historic periods. The Dear America series is another such example. What if, rather than writing about a fictional character, students were to write about a famous historical person? Most children have spent at least a small portion of their lives pretending to be someone like King Arthur or Princess Diana, Charles Lindbergh or Amelia Earhart.

Students all learn about American history while they are in grade school. Many historical figures are well known, but many are not. To write about historical characters, students must learn about the details of their lives: what they ate and wore, where they lived, how they traveled, what problems they had, and how they relaxed. Using the clues of what is known about a character, students can try to figure out what motivated that person. Finally, in order to write a play about that person, students must pretend and imagine. A play allows students to write from the first-person perspective, giving them the freedom to imagine they are all of the characters in the story, from the famous person to that person's best friend or co-worker.

Young students can not only read about our presidents, but they can also "become" them. Older students can "walk a mile in the shoes" of interesting people and better understand their accomplishments. Famous authors from our early history, such as Henry David Thoreau or Mark Twain, and painters like Winslow Homer or Frederic Remington are wonderful subjects for a play. Students can choose a state from which to find a famous character, for example, Jefferson Davis from Georgia or the Jesuit missionary Pierre Francois-Xavier de Charlevoix from Michigan.

Ask students what they want to be when they grow up and then have them find a person who pioneered the field. There are scientists like Albert Einstein, pilots like Charles Lindbergh, engineers like Edsel Ford, architects like Frank Lloyd Wright, and nurses like Florence Nightingale. The goal is to research one famous person and make him or her come alive in a play.

Young students can write a monolog in which the character explains either an important incident or a creation of their character. Imagine a classroom lined with diminutive political leaders who signed the Declaration of Independence, each stepping forward to make a brief speech about himself or his politics. Older students could write a dialog between those same politicians as part of a debate panel with set questions they have to answer in advance. Students could also arrange a fictional meeting between two people with similar interests, such as Teddy Roosevelt and Frederic Remington planning a fictional western hunting expedition. The possibilities are endless.

For this chapter, Paul Revere will come to the stage from our early history. His famous ride to Concord is well known, but by staging a play, students can imagine what went through his mind on that famous night. Several Internet sites will help shape a play.

Playwriting

Paul Revere's ride to Concord may be more legend than fact, but some things are clear. He was a good horseman, brave, and patriotic. There are many Web sites with information about Paul Revere. Dave Kleber (Kleber) explains some key parts of the traditional story on his Web page. For instance, he says Paul Revere would not have yelled "The British are coming" because he considered himself British. He would have called those soldiers British "regulars" because they were trying to apprehend the leaders of the opposition, namely Sam Adams and John Hancock.

Another site ("Letter") includes the text of a letter by Paul Revere to Dr. Jeremy Belknap, dated 1798. Revere called the enemy the "Tories." Perhaps he cried "The Tories are coming!" on his ride. In his letter, Revere described in detail what happened that night. He explained the signal in the North Church steeple, which a friend would light, and how information was passed from person to person. He named all the people he met, where they were, what was said, and what happened, all the way up to the point where he helped Sam Adams and John Hancock escape through the ranks of the militia and "the shot heard around the world" rang out at the beginning of the American Revolutionary war.

A third source of information about the incident is the long poem by Henry Wadsworth Longfellow, titled "Paul Revere's Ride," which is also available in its entirety online (Longfellow). Longfellow wrote his poem nearly one hundred years after the event in "an attempt to arouse patriotic feelings. He did not seek historical accuracy," according to the editor's note.

The incident took place over one night, a reasonable time for a play setting. A great deal of the action was on horseback. Will it be necessary to simulate that ride? That decision should follow others, such as whether to create a monolog from Longfellow's familiar poem, a readers theatre script from Revere's letter, or a play script that includes everything. Longfellow's poem is full of action and sound and would work well as the basis for a readers theatre piece, but we've already done that with "The Raven" in Chapter 7. While it might be entertaining to place a reader and sound master on stage to present the poem as if it were a radio performance, it might also be so comical watching the sound master that the sense of historical significance would be lost.

Instead, the challenge of creating a play script will be tackled. The first decision is to avoid the parts in the story that involve actually riding the horse. The ride may be memorable, but it is impractical to put on stage. The dialog occurred when Paul Revere met his compatriots and the regulars, so that is how the play will be framed. The main events will become scenes. First, Revere arranged for the signal. Second, he got a horse and began his ride. Third, he arrived in Lexington and warned Sam Adams and John Hancock so that they could avoid capture before the battle began. Fourth, soldiers captured him on the road to Concord and then he escaped. Fifth, he returned to Lexington as the first shot rang out. Those are the significant incidents. There are four stages: the North church tower in Boston, a stable yard, a house in Lexington, and the road to Concord.

To begin the story in the North Church tower (it wasn't considered old in those days), the actors will climb stairs onto the stage, and then lean over a railing to see the city and church yard below. Longfellow's description of that scene is very dramatic and can be used as a source for designing backdrops and lighting, while the emotions are revealed through dialog. We'll pull the actual names of Revere's coconspirators from his letter to Dr. Belknap and then listen as they make their plans. After Scene 1 an intermission will provide time for a scene change.

For Scene 2 we'll avoid the artistic license Longfellow took with the events (he describes Revere waiting by the river, rowing across alone, and then riding his own horse) and stick to the facts. We'll pick up the action as Revere borrows a horse from his friend Deacon Larkin and hears news from a lawyer, Richard Devens, about soldiers along the road to Lexington. It all takes place in a stable yard.

Scene 3 is at the home of the Reverend Mr. Clark in Lexington, where Sam Adams and John Hancock have been studying their maps and making plans. Revere delivers his warning. Scene 4 will take place in front of the stage, with a simple signpost to indicate it is the road to Concord. Daws and

Revere meet Doctor Prescott, who will help them spread the alarm. Daws and Prescott leave to warn one household, and redcoats capture Revere, although he soon escapes. Scene 5 is back at the Clark residence, as Revere and Mr. Lowell, Mr. Hancock's assistant, return to retrieve Mr. Hancock's trunk. They narrowly escape through the ranks of the militia as the redcoats arrive at the house and the first shots are fired.

Paul Revere's letter never once mentions any women in connection with these events. Three reasons lead to their introduction into this play. First, there would have been women in each location, in the homes and at the church, taking care of things as their husbands and brothers fought in the militia. Their part, though transparent to Paul Revere and Dr. Belknap, was very much a reality. Second, our intended middle school acting class will have young women who would like to participate. Finally, the style of the day was for men to wear their long hair in low ponytails. Therefore, it would be simplest to draw from the female population at the school for the many extras required as soldiers, if not also for some of the main characters. Appropriate names for these fictional characters will have to be chosen carefully, perhaps borrowed from famous literary or historical figures of the time.

How elaborate the three sets become will depend very much on the budget and time available to the actors and their tech support. Let's assume this will be a school production with a limited budget but with the labor of students in theater classes.

To create the church tower in Scene 1, two sections of stair railing are mounted on stands and used to indicate a corner of the tower. The action takes place at night so the rest of the stage is dark. A small, wooden cutout, made to resemble rooftops below the tower, is placed opposite the railing and along the back wall of the stage. A soft, bluish light directed at the cutout creates the effect of moonlight. If a light is unavailable, the cutout can be painted to look like it is lit by moonlight.

For Scene 2, the railing section is replaced with a split-rail fence section that is anchored by bales of hay and a hay fork. A saddle across the rail would be a perfect touch, but barring that, other riding gear can be carried or displayed to indicate the presence of a horse. A cutout of a large tree replaces the rooftops opposite the railing. The tree, fence, and saddle can also be painted onto a backdrop.

Scene 3 opens at the house of the Reverend Mr. Clark. A colonial dining room is created with a table and wooden chairs. Various colonial accessories such as a quilt, candlesticks, pewter platters, and so forth will set the period time frame. Scene 4 is the road to Concord, so a signpost is placed in front of the stage while the stage remains dark. Scene 5 returns to the Clark residence on stage.

Costumes are improvised except for the long, full skirts of the women characters, which need to be sewn or borrowed from costume shops. There is Martha Brown, an elderly woman with her hair in a bun who escorts the men up the stairs of the church belfry; Emily, a young farm maiden with a shorter skirt and her hair in two braids who is the daughter of Deacon Larkin; and finally Mrs. Clark, the wealthy wife of the Reverend Clark who harbors Sam Adams and John Hancock in Lexington. The "men" wear ponytails tied low with black ribbons, knee pants, and small pouches with the straps crisscrossed across their chests. These may also have to be sewn. The militia can't afford matching uniforms like the red coats, and they need to blend into the woods, so their clothing colors vary from brown to navy and black. The regulars or "redcoats" wear red shirts and tan knee pants. Knee pants are achieved by either cutting off an old pair of pants or rolling up the bottoms. Muskets can be fashioned from shaped pieces of painted wood, but a recording will be required or a backstage crew to make the sounds of battle.

The list of characters is assembled from the letter Revere wrote to Belknap, plus the fictional ladies. Take a look at *The Midnight Ride of Paul Revere.*

THE MIDNIGHT RIDE OF PAUL REVERE

Summary

This five-act play reveals the actions of the American patriot Paul Revere that preceded the first shot fired in the American Revolutionary war. While many accounts and paintings focus on Revere's strong and brave steed that carried him through the Massachusetts countryside, this play reveals the human encounters that shaped history. It is based on a letter Paul Revere sent to Dr. Jeremy Belknap in 1798, which is preserved by the Massachusetts Historical Society.

Set

Scene 1—the bell tower of the North Church in Boston. Two sections of railing set into stands create a corner of the tower. The rest of the stage is dark except for a wooden cutout designed to look like the moonlit rooftops of the houses of Boston. Scene 2—the stable yard of Deacon Larkin. A split-rail fence replaces the railing. A bale of hay, hay fork, and riding accessories complete the picture. Scene 3—the colonial dining room of the Reverend Mr. Clark: A wooden table covered with a quilt, wooden chairs, several candles and maps, a large trunk, and a water pitcher and bowl with towels. Scene 4—the road to Concord. A signpost placed in front of the stage points to Concord. Scene 5—returns to Mr. Clark's dining room.

Props

Muskets will be carried by British regulars as well as American militia. They are made out of shaped and painted wood. Spyglass for Colonel Conant. Water pitcher and bowl. Candles, maps, soup pot, teapot, a large trunk with two handles on the sides, a small black book.

Costumes

A long, full skirt, white blouse, and apron for Martha; a shorter dress and pinafore for Emily. Mrs. Clark wears a patriotic blue dress and a shawl crossed in front and tucked into her apron. Minutemen wear dark shirts and knee pants, pouches attached to dark straps that cross their chests, tan knee socks, and dark boots or shoes. The redcoats wear red shirts, tan knee pants, white strapped pouches, white knee socks, and dark boots or shoes. The minutemen wear black three-corner hats, while the redcoats wear tall, stiff red hats. Both types of hat can be fashioned out of construction paper. All "men" wear low ponytails tied with black ribbon, which may be bobby-pinned in place. Colonel Conant and Major Mitchell wear wooden sabers in a loop at their waist.

Characters

(Some of these characters are based on historical figures, others are fictional.)

Martha Brown	John Hancock
Paul Revere	Sam Adams
Dr. Warren	William Daws
Colonel Conant	Dr. Prescott
Emily Larkin *(Deacon Larkin's daughter)*	Major Mitchell
Deacon Larkin	British Regulars *(redcoats)*
Richard Devens, Esquire	Mr. Lowell
Reverend Mr. Clark	Old Tom
Mrs. Clark	American Militia

THE MIDNIGHT RIDE OF PAUL REVERE

Scene 1—North Church Bell Tower

(Martha Brown carries a candle and leads Paul Revere up the stage steps from the audience. Dr. Warren and Colonel Conant follow them.)

Martha Brown: Here we are, Mr. Revere. *(Blows out candle.)* You'll not need my candle from here, not with that moon lighting up the heavens. Watch your step. Isn't the view grand?

Revere: Yes, it is, Mrs. Brown. You are most kind to allow us access to the tower. We won't keep you waiting long.

Martha: Take your time, my dears. I'll be trimming the tapers downstairs for some time yet.

Warren: Give my regards to your husband, the Right Reverend Brown.

Martha: Thank you, Dr. Warren, I certainly will. *(Curtseys and exits back down stairs.)*

Warren: Mrs. Brown is a very conscientious woman. I am certain we can trust her discretion.

Conant: Yes, I agree. I've known her husband for years. Now then, let's take a look. *(Pulls out spyglass.)* Ah, a perfect clear night, and the moon is high. See how it reflects off the sea?

Revere: She's a wise woman as well. She blew out her candle before reaching the top to avoid giving away our position. Very clever of her, I'd say.

Conant: Yes, yes, very clever. Let's hand out ribbons when this is all over, not before it's even begun, shall we?

Revere: *(Clears throat.)* Yes, absolutely, Colonel Conant. *(Looks out over the railing in the opposite direction.)* I've determined that a light here is visible at the bend in the Charles River. The trees in the common shield the light from the regulars there.

Warren: It's true. I explored the entire common last night and could not see this tower from any vantage point.

Conant: Have you confirmed whether a light here is visible from the Charles, Mr. Revere?

Revere: Yes, but it is only visible from the far side, so I shall have a boat ready to get me across the river.

Conant: Excellent, gentlemen. What will the signal be?

Revere: Reverend Brown and his family will take turns in the tower. If they see a movement of ships toward the harbor they will light two lanterns and place them on this side of the tower. If the redcoats march, one lantern will shine.

Conant: Let me see if I understand correctly. One light if they come by land, and two if by sea?

Warren: That is correct, Colonel.

Conant: Then an express will be sent directly to Misters Hancock and Adams?

Revere: No sir, an express would surely be stopped within the city. I plan to watch at the bend in the Charles and then cross by boat and ride from the edge of town.

Warren: We have a network of riders, sir, who keep us posted on troop movements along the roads. They will help us choose our route.

Conant: What if the regulars position more ships along the Charles River? How will you pass the men-of-war?

Revere: My friends with the boat fish every night sir, so they are familiar to anyone who watches the river and will be considered harmless. I shall hide in the bottom of their boat.

Conant: Good and where will you hide your horse?

Revere: I'll not use my own horse, sir, but rather borrow one from my good friend Deacon Larkin.

Warren: Deacon is a good man, Colonel Conant. He also has the strongest steed in Boston. His holding on the edge of the city sees little traffic although there is a steady stream of visitors to the church. Another man among them will go unnoticed.

Conant: How many know this plan?

Warren: Only those of us who have been meeting at the Green Dragon Tavern. We are a small group and have all sworn an oath on the Bible that we would not reveal any information from our meetings except to you, Mr. Hancock, and Mr. Adams.

Conant: We must remain vigilant. Dr. Warren, what is your report on the troop movements in the common?

Warren: On Tuesday evening, a number of soldiers marched toward the bottom of the common. The road to Lexington starts there. Lexington is the headquarters of Mr. Hancock and Mr. Adams.

Revere: They've also lowered the boats that had been hauled aboard the men-of-war for repairs. The boats hang under the stern, ready for a quick launch.

Warren: The grenadiers and light infantry have been taken off duty.

Conant: Then they are preparing for an offensive. The time has come, my friends. I will alert the militia. We will stay under cover and await your signal. I will not start this conflict, but I will certainly take a hand in ending it. Godspeed. *(Exits down stairs.)*

Revere: Have you heard any more from Daws, Dr. Warren?

Warren: Yes, he has just returned from Lexington. Hancock and Adams are safe.

Revere: The time is near; I can feel it in my bones.

Warren: *(Looks toward the sea.)* There is a cold wind coming off the sea, a typical spring evening. At least it has blown away the clouds and given us an excellent view from here.

Revere: An excellent view of the graveyard, you mean.

Warren: No, Paul. Look at the city. The moonlight is so bright it could be daylight. Don't dwell on the bodies in the graveyard below.

Revere: There are so many, doctor, so many dead. Look at all those bodies, wrapped in silence and still. Yet the wind passes through the tents, steady as a sentinel.

Warren: Yes, and the wind says all is well. Remember those who have already died for our cause. Don't let them down. Many count on you.

Revere: Will Daws and I ride together, as planned?

Warren: Yes, with two riders there is a better chance to get through. To your post. I will pass by Deacon Larkin's home and ask him to prepare his horse.

Revere: A saddled horse is suspicious. Better to keep it well fed and watered. I can saddle him quickly enough when the time comes.

Warren: As you wish. Godspeed, young man.

Revere: Thank you. Be watchful as well and look after Mrs. Warren. I'll want more of her glorious ginger cakes one of these days.

Warren: *(Laughs.)* Good idea. That will keep her hands busy and ease her worries. Good night.

Revere: Good night. *(Lights down.)*

INTERMISSION

Scene 2—Deacon Larkin's Stable Yard

(Paul Revere enters from stage right, his eyes sweeping the stage and audience. Emily Larkin enters from stage left, carrying a bucket of water.)

Paul Revere: Good evening, Mistress Larkin. Is your father about?

Emily: Oh, Mr. Revere. This is all so exciting. Father sent me to water his horse and give him an extra portion of oats. Has it begun, then?

Revere: Now Emily Larkin, you know better than to ask me such questions. What if the redcoats interrogated you?

Emily: Why, I'd tell them to jump in the mud, I would. I'm not afraid of those stuffy regulars.

Revere: Stuffy? Where does a young lady learn such terms?

Emily: But they do look all stuffed like a feather bed after a good fluffing. They marched past here this morning with their chests all puffed out, their buttons shining, and boots polished like they were in a parade. They think they're so handsome and smart in their matching uniforms. Well, they're not. They're just silly little tin soldiers that should all be melted down and turned into good, useful plows.

Revere: You'd use them to turn your lettuce patch, Miss Emily?

Emily: I certainly would.

Revere: *(Laughs.)* How many plows marched by this morning?

Emily: Oh silly, they're not plows yet, just soldiers. Now let's see, there were six in a row and I counted ten rows, so that makes . . . sixty plows, I mean soldiers.

Revere: You've been practicing your sums, haven't you?

Emily: Yes.

Revere: Thank you, Miss Emily. I'll take that bucket of water for the horse, if you'll go tell your father I'm here. *(Exits stage right with bucket.)*

Emily: *(Curtseys and giggles.)* Yes, Mr. Revere. I'll be right back. *(Exits stage left. Moments later Deacon Larkin and Emily enter stage left.)*

Deacon Larkin: Emily, have you fed the horse yet?

Emily: No, Papa. Mr. Revere arrived before I could. I'll do it right away.

Richard Devens: *(Enters stage left.)* Good evening, Deacon Larkin. I bring news about the road to Lexington.

Larkin: Ah, your timing is perfect, Mr. Devens. That must be why you're on the Committee of Safety. Emily, say hello to Mr. Richard Devens, a lawyer from Boston.

Emily: *(Curtseys.)* Pleased to meet you, Mr. Devens. Please excuse me while I finish feeding the horse.

Devens: It's a pleasure to meet you as well, Miss Larkin. *(Emily exits.)* As for the Committee of Safety, Deacon, I suspect my frequent travels give me a good cover, nothing more.

Larkin: I don't know how many clients you have in the countryside, but the regulars are less likely to stop a lawyer such as you than a rough farmer. You manage an air of authority that probably intimidates them.

Devens: That's an old trick my father taught me. Act as if you belong somewhere and people will assume you do. It's simple really.

Larkin: Maybe you've missed your calling then. You would do well on stage.

Devens: Heaven forbid. My father, the judge, would roll in his grave.

Larkin: That settles it then. I'm sure you want to see young Revere. I'll go finish feeding the horse and send Revere out to hear your report. *(Exits stage right.)*

Devens: I'll keep an eye on the road in the meantime.

Revere: *(Enters, brushing hands off.)* Mr. Devens, you wish to see me?

Devens: It's a pleasure to meet you, Mr. Revere. *(They shake hands.)* I've heard so much about you. I was just with our friends, Hancock and Adams. They grow impatient.

Revere: Well, their wait is over. I've just come from the river; the signal lantern is lit. There were two of them, so they come by boat, floating in on the new tide. I should have expected it. Well, now it's done and I must spread the word.

Devens: Excellent. I noticed the light and that is why I came. I must warn you that I passed ten soldiers, all well mounted and armed on my return from Lexington.

Revere: When and where did you see the soldiers, Mr. Devens?

Devens: It was just at sundown and they were less than ten miles down the road, heading this way.

Revere: Ten soldiers are all marching this way? That's curious. Were there no roadblocks?

Devens: No, they rode at a leisurely pace, as if they were searching for something or someone.

Revere: Well, if they're looking for me, they'll have to be stealthier. Honestly, marching right down the middle of the road . . .

Devens: That's right.

Revere: Great. They'll be easy to spot and avoid.

Emily: *(Enters.)* Mr. Revere, the horse is saddled. Papa is holding him for you by the drinking trough. He said to give you these. *(Hands him a cloth napkin wrapped around biscuits.)*

Revere: *(Smells the bundle.)* Emily, are these fresh-baked ginger cakes?

Emily: *(Curtseys.)* Yes sir. I made them myself. I heard they're your favorite.

Revere: *(Takes her hand and kisses it.)* I thank you most sincerely, Miss Emily. They will bring me good luck tonight. I'm sure of it.

Emily: You're welcome. *(Curtseys again, exits giggling.)*

Revere: Thank you, for your report, Mr. Devens. Now, if you'll excuse me, I have a long night ahead of me. Good evening. *(Runs off stage right.)*

Devens: Godspeed, Mr. Revere. Our fate is in your hands. *(Exits.)*

INTERMISSION

Scene 3—Reverend Mr. Clark's House, Lexington

(Sam Adams and John Hancock study maps spread on a table. Enter Mrs. Clark, leading Paul Revere.)

Mrs. Clark: They're right in here, Mr. Revere. They've been studying those maps as if they were looking for treasure.

Revere: Thank you, Mrs. Clark. Ah, gentlemen, have you found the treasure?

Hancock: The treasure is all around you, Revere. Good people, handsome farms, woods teaming with life . . .

Adams: We just have to wrestle it from the grasp of those greedy, warmongering Tories.

Hancock: And if it's war they want, that's what they'll get. How was the road, Revere?

Revere: Teaming with redcoats. I came across two past Charlestown Neck. One tried to cut me off so I turned back and took a detour down the Medford road. He took off across a field and landed in the clay pond at the bend. I got into Medford all right.

Adams: Did they see you coming?

Revere: No, I had to awaken the captain of the minutemen who mustered the others. I must have roused every house between Medford and Lexington.

Hancock: Very good. There's water in the basin by the window. Adams, this man needs food and drink. Would you be so kind?

Adams: Yes, yes, I'll go. I can't look at those maps another minute. Perhaps we should gather them up, in case we have to make a hasty retreat. *(Exits.)*

Hancock: Good idea. I'll start rolling them and make room for our food.

Revere: *(Washing face and hands at the basin.)* I'll give you a hand in a minute. Which reminds me, have you heard from William Daws?

Hancock: No, should we have?

Revere: I thought he'd arrive before me. I had to wake people up. He rode on without stopping.

(Enter Adams and Daws. Daws carries bowls and spoons, Adams carries mugs.)

Adams: We were just packing up . . .

Revere: There you are. Where have you been?

Daws: Playing hide and seek with the redcoats. They nearly found me, but I slipped away. *(Enter Mr. Clark with a soup pot, Mrs. Clark with a teapot.)* Looks like I got here just in time for supper.

Adams: You've earned your keep tonight, Daws. Revere reports the regulars are on the move, and yet you avoided them.

Daws: Certainly. Luckily, their red coats light up like beacons in a full moon. They were easy to spot.

Revere: It's true. Their straps will make them easy targets for our muskets.

Hancock: Let's keep that information under our hats, gentlemen. We wouldn't want their tailor to learn of his mistake and ruin our advantage.

Adams: Our positions among the trees will be an even bigger advantage as they march their straight rows of men down roads and across our fields.

Hancock: We must remember, as we head into battle, that those targets are men. They are someone's sons, fathers, and brothers.

Daws: Yes, but their relatives are all in England.

Revere: . . . and they've gotten very greedy.

Mr. Clark: That's the truth. If I paid the taxes they demand I'd be ruined. I'd have to sell the house to come up with that much money.

Mrs. Clark: Gentlemen, please. Let's set aside our talk of war and pause a moment to remember our many blessings.

Hancock: Mrs. Clark, you make an excellent point.

Adams: That's right, let's talk about our gardens and grandkids while we eat. It will help ease digestion. Never mind the fact that our neighbors are gathering arms and huddling in the woods on a cold, damp night like this, while we sit here warm as wool mittens.

Hancock: Let us hope that thoughts of hearth and family keep our compatriots warm tonight.

Daws: There will be enough action to warm them soon enough. Thank you, Mrs. Clark, for this excellent stew.

Mr. Clark: My wife's stew is famous in Lexington.

Revere: As well it should be.

Adams: Madam, your cooking skills are only surpassed by your beauty.

Mr. Clark: *(Laughs.)* Mrs. Clark, I believe you have won another heart.

Mrs. Clark: Never fear, my dear. You won't sway my heart with sweet talk, Mr. Adams. Now, if you'll excuse me, I must return this pot to the hearth to keep it warm, in case any more express riders need fortifying. *(Exits.)*

Daws: Right. Well, I've had my fill. Shall we ride for Concord, Revere? There's many more to awaken before this night is over.

Revere: Concord it is, Daws. Keep your eyes on the road, Mr. Hancock. I shouldn't wait too long. The militia will be gathering at the meetinghouse and you can make your escape under cover of darkness for yet a few hours.

Hancock: We'll stay as long as possible.

Adams: Don't worry, Revere. We won't let them get their hands on us. You just ride fast and raise the alarm. The regulars won't even see us coming.

Revere: Very good then. Good night, gentlemen. *(Exits.)*

Daws: Hey, wait for me, Revere. Good night, gentlemen. *(Exits.)*

Hancock: Godspeed.

Adams: Keep your heads down.

Mr. Clark: I'd better finish cleaning my musket downstairs. Mrs. Clark hates to have the

Historical Plays

thing lying around her kitchen. Call if you spot any movement along the road. My son is watching from the woods about a quarter mile down.

Hancock: What will his signal be?

Mr. Clark: He'll howl like a coyote. He's been practicing it for weeks. Redcoats will be a coyote. Minutemen won't raise a peep. Excuse me. *(Exits.)*

Adams: Clever boy. Let's take another look at the road to Woburn, Hancock. I want to set it clearly in my mind as a contingency plan.

Hancock: Good idea. It's right here, the last one I rolled up. *(Spreads map on table and both study it. Lights down.)*

Scene 4—The Road to Concord

(Enter Revere and Daws at front of stage, curtains closed.)

Revere: Just over this hill we'll be able to see the bend in the road. We'll be able to see those white crossed straps from here.

Daws: It looks as still as death, too still for me. Shhh! Listen, someone's coming from behind us.

(Enter Dr. Prescott, holding up his hands, walking forward quietly.)

Dr. Prescott: Gentlemen, I bear you no ill will. I've come to warn you. I saw you leave Mr. Clark's home. I'm Dr. Prescott, and I am a High Son of Liberty.

Daws: Can you prove it?

Prescott: I have papers.

Revere: That's either a very brave or very stupid thing to carry tonight.

Prescott: It is a signature from Mr. Hancock in my patient register. *(Holds up a small black book.)*

Daws: Let me see that. *(Grabs it and flips pages.)*

Prescott: It's on the third to last page.

Daws: *(Laughs.)* That's Hancock, all right, curlicues and all.

Revere: *(Holds out hand to shake.)* Sorry about that, Doctor. I'm Paul Revere and this is William Daws.

Prescott: Think nothing of it, just tell me what's afoot. I wish to be of service.

Revere: We're raising the alarm from here to Concord, but we expect to meet road blocks at the main intersections like this one.

Daws: There was a company of ten on this road earlier this evening.

Revere: We expect them to split up and cover more corners at night.

Prescott: You intend to notify everyone along the road?

Daws: That's our job.

Prescott: Then let me join you. I know these people and they will give your news more credit if I am with you.

Revere: If that will speed our progress, then by all means . . . *(Points.)* I say we avoid that corner and cut across that field to the right.

Daws: I'll stop at the first house, you take the second.

Prescott: I'll go with you, Mr. Daws. That first house has several hounds who know me but may give you trouble.

Revere: Good, then we'll meet further down the road in a few minutes.

Daws: Keep your eyes open, Revere. *(Exits with Prescott.)*

Revere: . . . and your ears, Daws. *(Turns as if to leave, then stops. Enter two redcoats.)* Daws! Prescott! Look out!

Soldier: Silence! He's trying to alert others. Spread out. Find them.

(Enter two more redcoats who surround Revere, then turn their backs to him while looking around. Prescott enters, then exits quickly. Two soldiers follow and exit.)

Revere: *(Escapes in opposite direction, calls as exits.)* Hah—that's the way, doctor. Right over that wall. *(Backs into sight, followed by six more soldiers.)*

Soldier: Well, what have we here? A spy? What's your name?

Revere: Paul Revere.

Soldier: Where do you live?

Revere: Boston.

Soldier: What brings you to the Lexington road at this time of night?

Revere: I'm an express rider.

Soldier: What time did you leave Boston? *(Motions for two soldiers to grab Revere's arms.)*

Revere: I left at five o'clock, just as your ships ran aground in the river. They'll be surrounded by five hundred Americans by now, because I've alerted everyone from here to Boston.

Major Mitchell: *(Enters with authority.)* I see you've caught a rebel spy, gentlemen. Allow me to gently persuade him to sing. *(Pulls out a pistol and points it at Revere's head.)* Mr. Paul Revere, I am going to ask you some questions, and if you do not answer them truthfully, I will blow your brains out. Your name?

Revere: Paul Revere.

Mitchell: Your home?

Revere: Boston.

Mitchell: Your business tonight?

Revere: An express.

Mitchell: Silence! *(Pats Revere's sides, searching for weapons.)* Not even a pistol to defend yourself from bandits?

Revere: They can't catch me.

Mitchell: *(Turning to his men.)* This insolent scum will be our new guide. If his friends are filling the woods as he says, they will hesitate to shoot. *(Sneers at Revere.)* Take us to Lexington, Mr. Express. Sergeant, shoot this man if he tries to escape or if you hear a peep from his friends in the woods.

Soldier: Yes, sir!

(All slowly march toward exit. Loud boom as several guns are discharged off stage. All freeze.)

Mitchell: Keep your eyes and ears open, men. They are drawing near. Revere, how much further to Cambridge?

Revere: You're at least twenty miles away.

Mitchell: Is there another road?

Revere: Nope. This is it. You won't get far on any road tonight. Our minutemen are already gathering.

Mitchell: *(Sneers.)* Colonials. Sergeant, come here. Is your horse tired?

Soldier: Yes sir, he is, sir.

Mitchell: Take Revere's horse; we will ride fast to Lexington. Leave Revere here, he'll just slow us down, and I don't trust him. Let's go! *(Leads other soldiers off stage at a run.)*

Revere: Horse thieves! *(To himself.)* Perfect! This is the burying ground, and those pastures lead right to the Reverend Mr. Clark. It's time his house guests found new lodgings. *(Exits opposite to soldiers.)*

Scene 5—The Reverend Mr. Clark's House

(Hancock and Adams are again at the table. Revere rushes in.)

Revere: Gentlemen, I believe things are about to heat up out there.

Adams: What are you talking about? You were just here, what happened?

Revere: I just met a company of regulars who held a gun to my head and made me lead them to Lexington. They got spooked when our militia discharged their muskets up at the meetinghouse. You should have seen those redcoats run.

Hancock: Our men are gathering, taking their places in the woods. That company won't get far.

Revere: That's what I told them.

Hancock: *(Laughs.)* Revere, you like to live dangerously. *(Stomps feet twice on floor.)*

Revere: You'll experience the thrill of it if you stay here any longer. Now what do you need to take.

Adams: We're ready to go, horses are saddled in the barn. *(Enter Mr. Lowell.)*

Mr. Lowell: Yes, Mr. Hancock? What can I do for you?

Hancock: Take these papers in your satchel. It's time for us to ride.

Adams: To Woburn then?

Hancock: That is our plan.

Revere: I'll go with you, run interference, if necessary.

Hancock: Your guidance is most welcome, young Mr. Revere.

(All exit. Lights down. Pause before Revere and Lowell return.)

Revere: Now where did you say that trunk was, Lowell?

Lowell: It's under the window, yes, here it is. *(Tugs trunk into room.)*

Revere: *(Takes a handle and helps Lowell lift the trunk.)* I see why you requested my help. This thing is heavy. What's in it?

Lowell: Books and papers. Mr. Hancock never travels without them. I shouldn't have left them behind.

Revere: We'll get them to him, don't worry.

(Enter Old Tom, carrying a musket.)

Old Tom: What's all the rushing around for, young sirs?

Revere: The redcoats are on the move, Tom. We have to get Adams and Hancock to safety.

Tom: Balderdash! I just left the tavern where a man came in from Boston. He said he didn't see any British troops on the road.

Revere: Well he was either a British spy or a blind man, Tom. I've run into plenty of soldiers tonight.

Lowell: *(A coyote howl is heard offstage.)* Quiet! I hear something. *(Another howl is heard.)* Look! *(Points offstage.)* There's movement down the hill past the rocks . . .

Revere: *(Looking in the same direction.)* . . . And if those aren't regulars marching in formation down there across that pasture, I'm not Paul Revere.

Tom: *(Looks as well.)* Well, I'll be darned. You can't miss those white straps and trousers, now, can you? That feller was mistaken. Now you gentlemen have business to take care of, I can see that. You just let me cover your exit and old Tom will consider himself lucky.

Revere: You won't be alone for long, Tom. Our militia will be here any minute. Come on, Lowell. Let's move.

Lowell: You lead, I have this end.

Revere: Tom? Do you know how to use that musket?

Tom: Of course I do, I've been hunting in these woods since I was a boy. I'm the best shot in the whole darned town.

Revere: Then we're lucky you came along. Keep your head down, will you?

Tom: Go on, get out of here. Old Tom can take care of himself. *(Raises musket and aims offstage, as Revere and Lowell exit. Lights down. Pause, then several minutemen enter furtively in front of stage, stop in staggered formation, kneel on one knee and take aim. Revere and Lowell run from the opposite direction, carrying the trunk, keeping their heads down.)*

Revere: *(Slows to a walk.)* Good evening, gentlemen. Pleasant night for a stroll. *(Gunshot sound offstage.)*

Minuteman: *(Laughs.)* Just keep your head down, Revere. We've got you covered. *(Another shot is heard.)*

Lowell: Quit joking around, Revere. Those aren't peashooters.

Revere: No, they're muskets carried by brave and patriotic Americans. We'll show those Tories. *(More gunshots as Revere and Lowell exit. Minutemen yell as they rush offstage to the sound of many gunshots.)*

References

Kleber, Dave. *Paul Revere's Ride*, January 16, 2003. http://www.city-net.com/~davekle/revere.htm.

Longfellow, Henry Wadsworth. "Paul Revere's Ride." James Madison University, Madison, Wisconsin. January 16, 2003. http://www.jmu.edu/madison/revere.htm.

Paul Revere "Letter." Massachusetts Historical Society Proc., XVI, 371–374. February 5, 2003. http://www.masshist.org/cabinet/April2002/reveretranscription.htm.

10

Cultural Myth Plays

Story Adaptation

For this chapter, students will begin with some research into cultural mythology. This is a great excuse for students to learn about a foreign country in greater depth than they can from school textbooks or encyclopedias. A culture's mythological stories explain what kind of people are heroes or villains in their society. The stories reveal characters who have influenced the thoughts and ideals that formed the country. They describe places that the country considers important, as well as climate, food, political structures, and forces.

Libraries are full of myth collections from various cultures such as Celtic, Roman, Norse, Japanese . . . you get the picture. Scholars like Joseph Campbell have made careers out of the study of myths, looking for differences and similarities between cultures. That is not what we're looking for. Our research should lead us to the stories of a particular culture.

What do stories such as the Celtic myth of Tristan and Iseult say about their culture? One account describes how when Tristan was wounded in war, Iseult rushed by ship to treat him with a magic cure. He died of his wound before she arrived because of a mistaken signal. She quickly died afterwards of a broken heart. Tristan was a valiant soldier; Iseult was a healer. Her love was so strong that without Tristan, Iseult's heart broke and she died. Their story reveals that in their culture ideal characteristics were love, loyalty, valor, and compassion.

This story was familiar to Shakespeare when he wrote *Romeo and Juliet.* Shakespeare recognized in the myth all the elements of a good story. He modernized it by changing the battle from English Celts and French Britons to a feud between Italian families. He knew battle scenes drew audiences because they are exciting and scary all at once. The cause of the feud in his play is unknown and unimportant. The important thing is how people make decisions about love and loyalty. Iseult's love was so strong that she risked the perils of war to deliver a cure. Shakespeare adjusted the story so that Juliet risked her family's anger for Romeo's love, and the potion was a sleeping one to mislead Romeo's family, not a cure. Juliet was also misled, which led to tragedy. Shakespeare's story included the dangers of deception and misplaced family loyalty.

That is why writers adapt new stories from old ones. It is because the characters love, fight, and die in heroic ways that remind us of our ideals. Myths often include gods with super powers and whose actions affect things people have no control over, such as the Norse god Thor with his lightning bolts and thundering hammer. Many early cultures have myths that help them explain their weather.

According to a recent article in *National Geographic* (Theroux, 5), Hawaiians are "struggling to reclaim their culture," so we will explore Hawaiian mythology as a means to understand their ideals. A search through the library turned up several picture books based on Hawaiian myths as well as collections that contain a single Hawaiian story. The reference page at the end of this chapter lists those sources.

The Silver Treasure contains one Hawaiian myth called "The Pig That Goes Courting." (McCaughrean, 81) It describes a relationship between two Hawaiian gods: Pele, the goddess of fire and volcanoes, and Kamapua'a. Kamapua'a was a god with the body (and manners) of a pig but the hands and feet of a human. He also had connections with water spirits. He fell in love with Pele, who tried to chase him away with insults. When those didn't work she threw lava rocks, and finally hot magma. He persisted, calling up his water friends, who created a great wall of mist. When Pele and her relatives finally grew tired of insulting Kamapua'a (and their volcanoes died down to mere grumbles), she stumbled down the mountain through the mists and he was waiting. He convinced her to give in and marry him, and soon her passion for him was as fiery as her temper had been.

This story sounds suspiciously like another Shakespeare play, *The Taming of the Shrew,* which he also set in Italy. We won't let that stop us from adapting this story into an even more modern love story. We will keep the personalities of the Hawaiian deities and modernize their powers. Their fiery relationship will become a metaphor for the struggle Hawaiians are having to reclaim their culture. We will borrow names and places from the myths and yet create original fictional characters that interact in a similar way.

Playwriting

Let's begin by describing the main characters. How would one create a man who is a pig for the stage? What if Kamapua'a is a sloppy young man? His clothes are dirty and torn (he's a pig) and he works as a dishwasher (his water friends) in a restaurant on the beach. Since the restaurant is only open at night, he spends all day surfing and flirting with the tourists on the beach. Most of the girls ignore him until they see him surfing. Then he wins their hearts with his skill and daring. His nickname is Ama.

Pele is a beautiful hula dancer. She is used to chasing away suitors every evening when she leaves work and has developed a fiery (volcanic) temper. Her troupe dances on a beach away from town, so it is not until Ama takes a vacation and goes to her beach to surf that they finally meet. She takes an instant disliking to him, while he falls in love. She calls on her relatives in the dance troupe, the ones who juggle with fire, to discourage him. He soothes her by pouring kind compliments over her. She shouts at him to leave.

A storm approaches and rumbles are heard from the local volcano, representing how Kamapua'a calls up his water spirit friends and how Pele rouses her volcanic relatives. Ama buys Pele a cool fruit drink (more water to soothe her) at the end of her dance. She tastes it and it is delicious and refreshing, but she throws it at him. He returns the next night and offers another drink decorated with a beautiful flower. She pours it out after several sips, looking him right in the eye, but tucks the flower into her hair. He returns a third night and offers her a drink in a coconut with a flower and paper umbrella.

Lightning flashes through the sky as waves build and crash on the beach. This time Pele is very thirsty, so she finishes the entire drink and finds a coral necklace in the bottom of the coconut. She returns it to Ama, but during the argument over whether she should keep it or not, he convinces her to try it on and wins her heart with his soft words and generosity. They run hand in hand laughing into the surf as the sky clears and the rumbles from the volcanoes fade away.

All of this can happen in two places. First there will be the restaurant on the beach, where Ama works. He will arrive at work, carrying a surfboard. He stops to flirt with a tourist and we learn about his dishwashing job and surfing skill. At the end of this scene, he announces he will be gone a week as he competes in a surfing competition on the far side of the island.

The second place is another beach filled with competing surfers, where a luau has been arranged to feed everyone at the end of the day. Of course, Pele's troupe will provide the entertainment. Costumes are beachwear and sarongs in bright Hawaiian colors and florals. Pele wears the traditional grass skirt.

The first set will have a palm-roofed archway that separates the beach and some lounge chairs from a small outdoor table with chairs at the restaurant. The stage floor is covered with sand. A painted backdrop shows the beach curving away into the distance with palm trees dotting a shoreline filled with high-rise hotels. In the second set, the arch is removed and a crowd enters with beach towels that they form into a circle. Musicians will play a guitar and bongo drums. The backdrop is exchanged for one that shows a beach curving in the opposite direction with a palm tree-covered mountain rising steeply toward a volcano. To avoid having to build a roasting pit on the stage, it can be painted into the backdrop. A surfboard will be one of Ama's props, as well as the flowers, coconut drink, and paper umbrella. This play is called *Fire and Water*.

FIRE AND WATER

Summary

A young Hawaiian finds true love when he meets a tempestuous hula dancer. Will he be able to win her heart? Will he have to change his slovenly ways? This play borrows its characters from the love story of Pele, the Hawaiian goddess of fire and volcanoes, and Kamapua'a, a god with the body of a pig and the hands and feet of a human.

Set

The stage floor is covered with a thin layer of sand. Two backdrops are painted. The first shows a beach curving into the distance to the left and dotted with small palm trees in front of a resort town filled with high-rise hotels. There is a palm-roofed arch at center stage that separates the beach, lined with three outdoor lounge chairs, from a small outdoor table with chairs. The arch has a hand-painted sign that reads Ka-uni's Kafe. The second backdrop shows a beach curving to the right and backed by a towering tree-covered mountain, topped with a volcano. There is a pig roasting in a pit down the beach. Three surfboards (or cutouts that look like boards) are cut in half and propped up on stage to look like they're buried in the sand.

Props

Surfboards, TV camera, beach towels, coconut half, long drinking straw, tiny paper umbrella, several flowers, and a coral necklace. Bongo drums, guitar case. A microphone for John Ho. Water bottles (one for cameraman, one for Ama). Punia carries on a tall glass of pink juice. A mug, a flower lei.

Costumes

Ama wears a brightly colored Hawaiian bathing suit, a T-shirt, and sandals in the first scene. He only needs the bathing suit in the second scene. Pele wears a bikini top and grass skirt, with flowers in her hair. Most others wear bright Hawaiian shirts, bathing suits, sarongs, flip-flops. John Ho wears a loose white shirt, Lee wears a photographer's vest.

Characters

Ama *(a Hawaiian surfer/dishwasher)*
Ashley *(a tourist)*

Greg *(Ashley's boyfriend)*
John Ho *(a TV sports reporter)*
Lee *(his cameraman)*
Pele *(a Hawaiian hula dancer)*
Punia *(Ama's cousin)*
Ricky *(Pele's brother)*
Larry *(a bongo drummer)*

FIRE AND WATER

Scene 1—A Day at the Beach

(Ama enters at a run from stage right, carrying his surfboard. The Beach Boys' song "T-bird" fades after playing the line, ". . . and we'll have fun, fun, fun . . .". Ashley and Greg are sunbathing in the lounge chairs.)

Ama: Hey, Punia, wait up!

Ashley: *(Waves and calls with a sing song voice.)* Hi, Ama. Where've you been all day?

Ama: *(Skids to a stop and leans on surfboard.)* Hi, Ashley. You're looking fine today. That a new bikini? *(Greg sits up and shades his eyes to see Ama.)*

Ashley: What? This old thing? I've had it for hours!

Ama: Did you go to my sister's shop like I told you?

Ashley: I think so, it was the one with all the suits on tables outside, right on the corner.

Greg: All the shops have suits outside on tables.

Ama: Hi, Greg.

Greg: S'up, dude?

Ama: My sister's shop is in the middle of the block.

Ashley: Oh, well, I tried.

Greg: She tried on nearly every suit in Hawaii. I almost got heatstroke, but did she care?

Ashley: Quit being such a martyr, Greg. So, Ama, didn't you say your sister's name was Lani?

Ama: That's right. Did you meet her?

Ashley: I met four Lani's. I bet you don't even have a sister. They all knew *you*, though.

Ama: *(Smiles and shrugs shoulders.)* What can I say? I have a big family.

Ashley: You're pulling my leg, right?

Ama: No, but I'd like to.

Greg: Down boy.

Ashley: Oh, cut it out, Greg!

Greg: Ama seems to be forgetting whose girlfriend you are.

Ashley: How could he forget? You're practically glued to my side.

Greg: If you'd quit flirting with every guy on the beach, I wouldn't have to be glued.

Ama: Uh, excuse me, I gotta go . . .

Cultural Myth Plays

Ashley: Don't go, he's harmless.

Greg: Let him go, Ashley. His buddies are waiting.

Ama: Yeah, that Punia's already catching a wave. I only have time for one ride before work. See ya! *(Exits.)*

Ashley: *(Watchs Ama leave.)* Now look what you did. You chased him away. Why do you have to go all macho and protective like that?

Greg: *(Lays back and closes eyes.)* You're imagining things. I don't have a macho bone in my body—you broke them all.

Ashley: I broke them all? Now you're being dramatic. *(Sighs and lies back with eyes closed.)* It's not like I want to go out with him or anything.

Greg: Of course not, that'd be the day. The day you date a dishwasher is the day I'll . . .

Ashley: Get a life?

Greg: Thanks. My ego just flickered out.

Ashley: I'm thirsty.

Greg: There'll be a waiter along any minute.

Ashley: *(Looking toward Ama.)* That's true. I can wait.

Greg: Where do you want to go for dinner tonight?

Ashley: Let's just stay here and eat at Ka-uni's.

Greg: Again? That would be the third time this week. I'm sick of greasy burgers.

Ashley: I'm too tired to go back to our room and get dressed. You could order a salad.

Greg: Rabbit food? No, thanks. I feel like fish.

Ashley: Don't they serve any here?

Greg: I'll ask Ama when he comes back.

Ashley: *(Still watching Ama.)* Here he comes now. Hey, Ama! How fast were you going?

Ama: *(Enters, shaking water from hair.)* Who knows? You'd need one of those radar guns to find out, but it's not like there's a speed limit out there. All I know is it was fast!

Ashley: I'll say. You were like a blur.

Greg: *(Mumbles.)* That's because you won't wear your glasses.

Ama: What's that? You want a glass of something? I'll send Tony out here.

Ashley: Oh, sure, that would be great. What did you say you wanted, Greg?

Greg: I'll take a soda.

Ama: Same as usual, eh? No problem, coming right up. Hey, you guys coming to tomorrow's competition?

Ashley: What competition?

Greg: The one he told you about every day this week.

Ashley: Oh, right. I'm not used to keeping track of things without my PDA. I'm on vacation, after all.

Greg: You just want to hear Ama talk.

Ama: *(Laughs.)* Yeah, right, but it's good you can relax. Don't worry about how to get there. Just tell any taxi driver on the island you want to see the surfer's cup tomorrow and they'll get you there.

Greg: Probably by the scenic route.

Ama: Hey, it's all scenic, man. Listen, I have to go. Ka'uni's making faces at me from the shack. He looks like some kind of volcano about to blow. *(Waves and smiles toward stage right.)* See you guys tomorrow. *(Exits.)*

Greg: Sure, tomorrow. Maybe we can find some seafood on the other side of the island.

Ashley: Greg, you know I can't eat seafood. I'm allergic.

Greg: You came all the way to Hawaii, in the middle of the Pacific, and you can't eat seafood?

Ashley: I'd go for another one of those pig roasts, though.

Greg: If I eat any more pork I'm going to grow a curly tail.

Ashley: It would look cute on you.

Greg: Sure, it would match my snout, right?

Ashley: . . . and your bristly chin.

(Lights fade, both exit.)

INTERMISSION

Scene 2—The Surfing Competition

(Lights rise on John and Lee recording a spot for the TV sports newscast. Lee shifts camera from stage right to John.)

John: *(Smoothes hair and faces camera.)* . . . and ready. Aloha Hawaii. This is John Ho, reporting live from the beach where the first day of the surfer's cup competition has been going on for several hours already. The rain predicted for this afternoon has yet to arrive, but the storm system moving in has created some hair-raisingly tall waves. *(Smoothes hair, laughs.)* The wind isn't helping much either. I've managed to snag one of the surfers to give us a rundown on the competition. His name is Kamapua'a. He is one of our local heroes, our hometown champion, and he has a large gathering of fans cheering him on from the beach. *(Sounds of cheering from offstage.)* Here he comes now.

Ama: *(Enters at a loose jog. Slicks wet hair back, then holds out hand to shake.)* Hey, John.

John: Hello, Kamapua'a . . .

Ama: Please, call me Ama.

John: You don't like your given name? Aren't you named after an ancient Hawaiian god who was a great lover?

Ama: Yeah, and he was, you know, a pig. Let's just say I got plenty of teasing over the years.

John: *(Laughs.)* I can only imagine. Okay, Ama it is then. So, tell us, what's it like out there today?

Ama: It's awesome, dude. The waves are totally bi— Oh, uh, sorry dude, I mean . . . really fast.

John: Can you tell us who is in the lead or is it too early to tell?

Ama: Me, of course. *(Smiles and waves at the camera, nodding.)* Hi mom, dad. *(Nods more.)*

John: Is that official?

Ama: Yeah, sure, I mean, I'm still here, haven't fallen or gone through the grinders . . .

John: Are you saying there are already some injuries?

Ama: Yeah, man . . . *(Turns suddenly serious.)* That is, a couple of *haoles,* like, totally crashed into each other. They were taken out in a chopper. That slowed things down, but . . .

John: They both survived, then?

Ama: I guess so, I don't know. They were pretty messed up. One of their boards split in two? . . . and it nearly speared my cousin, Punia? . . . but he swerved away and finished his ride like nothing doin', you know?

John: That's amazing. Were you out there too?

Ama: Oh, no, man. That's why I know what happened. I saw the whole thing from the beach. One guy lost it and fell off backwards, his board went like, right into another guys' board, knocking him off and splitting his board like it was balsa wood or something. So there's Punia, but he's like whoa! So then, he like, shot outta there.

John: Well, thank you Ama. *(Ama nods, waves to the camera, and lopes off.)* So, there you have it folks. Two surfers have already been eliminated from the competition this afternoon, taken out with injuries. Our local talent is full of confidence and the waves are really fast. This is John Ho, reporting live from the Surfer's Cup. Now back to you, Rhonda. *(Pauses and then nods to camera.)* That's a wrap, Lee. I'm going back to the van.

Lee: *(Lowers camera.)* You go ahead, I have to get some shots of the water and surfers for the late news, before it gets too dark.

John: Just don't get caught out here in the rain.

Lee: It's okay, I have the cover in my pocket. *(Pats the bulging pocket.)*

John: All right. I saw a soda stand on our way out, you want anything?

Lee: No thanks, I have my water. *(Pulls out a bottle from another pocket.)* How long do we get to stay out here?

John: I'll call in and see if it's a slow news day. Maybe we can stick around.

Lee: I'm game. Did you see the hula dancers arrive? They were heading over to the pig roast. I saw some musicians following them. Looks like a party is cooking up.

John: Hula?

Lee: Hula, pig roast, music, girls in grass skirts . . . swaying . . . you sure you have to check in?

John: Hey, I don't make the rules. How many pig roasts can you go to anyway?

Lee: It's not the pig, it's the dancers. You should have seen them, man. *(Sounds of bongo drums offstage.)*

John: All right, all right. Put your tongue back in your head and get your beach shots. Why don't you head whichever way you saw the hula girls going and I'll find you after I clear it with the office.

Lee: Sounds good to me. *(Exits stage right.)*

John: *(Calls out.)* Just watch where you're going . . . *(Flinches then laughs.)* How could you miss her? She's like a mountain, man. Oh, I see . . . yeah, yeah . . . that one's a looker all right. *(Laughs, shaking head and exits stage left. Drums get louder then subside as Ashley and Greg enter, carrying beach towels.)*

Ashley: Come on, Greg. They're starting.

Greg: Do we have to go to another pig roast? I thought we were just going to watch the surfing and then go find a restaurant.

Ashley: Aw, come on. We're here, the party's here, where's the problem?

Greg: The problem is I smell a pig.

Ashley: I smell pineapple, coconut, sunscreen, and salt water. Come on, the music's starting. *(Music flares, exits.)*

Greg: I'm coming. I just can't get enough of those hula girls . . . *(Pauses as Pele in grass skirt takes a couple of dance steps on stage, then dances off.)* Hello . . . now there's a hula girl I could watch all night. *(Runs after Pele.)*

Scene 3—A Close Encounter

(Enter Pele, carrying a bongo drum, followed by Ama.)

Ama: Slow down, dream boat. At least tell me your name.

Pele: *(Stops in a huff, spins to face him, stamping foot.)* First, I'm not your dream boat, and second I don't give my name out to customers.

Ama: I'm not a customer, I'm a surfer. I was competing today. Didn't you see me?

Pele: Were you watching our dance? *(Ama nods.)* You're a customer.

Ama: But I'm only here because of the competition.

Pele: Then you didn't like my dancing?

Ama: You dance like a goddess.

Pele: You're still a customer, and you smell like a pig.

Ama: That's because I had to sit where the smoke was blowing from the roasting pit.

Pele: Then you're not only a customer, but a stupid one.

Ama: I'm stupid for love of you and your grass skirt and your midnight black hair . . . *(Hovers close as if trying to smell her hair.)*

Pele: I'm probably only the fiftieth girl you've hit on since dinner. Get out of my way.

Ama: Let me carry that drum. You must be tired.

Pele: I'm tired of listening to you, that's for sure. Ricky! *(Searches for Ricky over Ama's shoulder.)* Where did you park the van? Oh great, now Ricky's talking to some blond haole. We'll be here for hours.

Ama: I'd give you a ride, but I don't have a car. I do . . . however . . . *(Looks toward Ricky.)* know those *haoles*. You want a ride with them? *(Waves over shoulder.)* Hi Ashley, Greg.

Pele: *(Shudders.)* Not for a million dollars, especially if they're friends of yours.

Ama: How about . . . *(Waves Punia over as he enters with a tall glass of pink juice. Takes it and offers it to Pele.)* . . . a glass of the sweetest nectar on this side of the island.

Pele: You are too kind. *(Takes glass, pours drink onto sand and tosses glass over shoulder.)*

Ama: Hey, what did you do that for?

Pele: I don't accept drinks from complete strangers.

Ama: I'm Ama, this is my cousin, Punia. Tell me your name and we won't be strangers.

Pele: In your dreams, stinky man. Ricky! Come on!

(Enter Ricky, carrying guitar cases and talking to Ashley.)

Ricky: Gimme a break, Pele. What's the rush? Oh, I see. Are these guys giving you trouble?

Pele: Of course they are, just like every night. There are some in every crowd.

Ricky: Back off, guys. You don't want to mess with my sister. She has a temper on her like you wouldn't believe.

Pele: Ricky!

Ricky: *(Laughs and shrugs.)* Take a hike, man. She's not for you.

Pele: You can say that again. *(Exits.)*

Ricky: She's not for you.

Ama: Hey, that's funny, man. Do you do everything she tells you?

Ricky: Sure, why not? I've even been known to drop my fire wands near audience members who look too interested in my sister, no charge.

Ashley: *(Takes Ama's arm.)* Do you have any idea who you're talking to? This is the best darned surfer this side of Australia, and I ought to know.

Ricky: What, you know this bum?

Ashley: He's only my best friend on this whole island.

Greg: Hey, what about me?

Ashley: Oh, silly, I mean besides you.

Ricky: Well, I don't care if he's your best friend in the whole world, Blondie. He needs to take a hike. *(Lunges at Ama, threatening.)*

Ama: *(Sarcastic.)* Whoa! Dude! I'm like, so scared. *(Waves to someone offstage and calls out.)* Come on, Punia. Our work here is done. Hey, Pele . . . see you around! *(Ricky fakes chasing him off, Ama puts his hands up, laughing, and backs off. Exit Ricky. Enter Punia.)* That's it. I'll never look at another girl as long as I live.

Punia: I think that's a medical impossibility.

Ashley: What about me?

Greg: *(Takes Ashley's arm and leads her offstage.)* If he so much as breathes in your direction . . . *(Ashley resists, looking over her shoulder at Ama as both exit.)*

Ama: I may look, but I won't see. I'll only see Pele. She's burned into my eyes and all the way into my heart. I'm on fire, man.

Punia: Yeah, you've got it bad, but it's not the first time and it probably won't be the last.

Ama: No, really. I'm done, finished, dead in the water, no good to any other woman from now on.

Punia: . . . as if you were any good before. I'm going to bed. The camper's right over here. You coming?

Ama: *(Shakes head as if clearing it.)* Why not? Tomorrow's another day. She'll be back. Her troupe's booked here all week. Did you see that busload of tourists they brought over from the city? I felt like a zoo exhibit, today.

Punia: You can't fool me, you loved every minute of it.

Ama: Maybe if they all looked like Pele, but those blue-haired ladies in straw hats and muumuus and their men with the knobby, hairy knees, black socks in sandals, and shiny pink heads . . . *(Shudders.)* They give me the creeps.

Punia: *(Yawns.)* Well I say it's time to creep into bed. I'm beat.

Ama: I may never sleep again.

Punia: If you don't sleep, how can you dream about her?

Ama: Now there's a thought. Okay, I'm coming. *(Both exit.)*

Scene 4—When Sparks Fly

(The stage lights darken, lightning flashes, thunder rolls, lights flash behind the volcano backdrop to make it look active. Enter Pele tugging on a sweater, followed by Ricky.)

Pele: This is ridiculous. We shouldn't have to perform when a storm is coming.

Ricky: You won't be cold for long. You dance right by the fire, but watch your skirt. You got so close last night, I thought you'd catch fire.

Pele: It's very hard to be graceful when you're covered in goose bumps.

Ricky: You know it's not up to me. Uncle Ed will call it off only if he thinks rain will ruin the drums.

Pele: He hasn't seen what rain can do to a grass skirt.

Ricky: *(Pauses, looking offstage.)* Well, well … look who's here. If it isn't your new boyfriend.

Pele: What? I don't have any boyfriends.

Ricky: That's because you're so nasty.

Pele: You're nasty.

Ricky: I may be overprotective, but I'm not nasty.

(Enter Ama with a steaming mug and a fresh lei.)

Ama: There you are. I was beginning to think you weren't coming tonight.

Pele: The thought did cross my mind.

Ama: I thought you might be cold, so I brought you a mug of hot tea.

Pele: *(Mimics, sarcastic.)* I thought you might be cold, so I brought you a mug of hot tea.

Ricky: That's my sweet, loveable, kind, gentle …

Pele: Drop it! *(Ama drops mug.)* Not you, idiot! I was talking to Ricky. Oh, man, what a waste.

Ama: No harm done. I'll just go get another one.

Pele: No time. I have to go on in minutes. *(Points at lei.)* Who's that for?

Ama: The most beautiful dancer on the beach.

Pele: You're kidding me. I can't accept that.

Ama: I was hoping you would, but if you don't want it, I'll just find someone else … *(Looks around. Enter Ashley and Greg.)* Hi guys, you still here?

Greg: Wild horses couldn't keep her away.

Ashley: I just love watching the surfers, and the sunsets aren't bad either.

Ama: *(Holds out lei.)* Here, this is for you.

Pele: *(Grabs lei.)* You said it was for me. I can't wear it, but I can use one of these for my hair. *(Plucks a flower off and tucks it behind ear, then offers lei to Ashley.)* There, you can tell all your friends that a Hawaiian surfer boy loves you and gave you this as a token of his affection.

Greg: *(Grabs lei.)* If anyone's going to give my girl a lei, it will be me.

Ashley: Greg, you're disgusting.

Greg: What? Now you don't want flowers?

Ama: Go ahead, Ashley. Wear them. They will bring you good fortune, even if they're missing a flower.

Ashley: Well, if you say so. I wouldn't want to turn down good fortune. *(Puts them on while making a face at Pele. Drums sound offstage.)* Come on Greg, we won't get a good seat if we mess around here any more. *(Exits with Greg.)*

Ricky: Speaking of messing around . . . I have to get set up. You coming, Pele? *(Exits.)*

Pele: As soon as this nuisance gets out of the way.

Ama: *(Steps aside.)* As you wish, my love.

Pele: Oh sure, as long as Blondie over there is out of the picture, I'm your love? You're a fickle flirt who's full of himself. Fly away, fool. We're finished.

Ama: Unfair! Fate made me find you, now I am a fool in love. We merely need to make it official.

Pele: Fine, we're officially finished.

Ama: I'm too much a fool to understand finished, especially when we've begun so well. Farewell for now, my fine filly.

Pele: If I'm a horse, you're a pig.

Ama: Yes, wallowing in wanton words, the better to woo you, my dear.

Pele: A pig and a wolf.

Ama: I'll be the whole animal kingdom for you if you want, only meet me after your dance and share another mug of tea.

Pele: A wolf in sheep's clothing is still a wolf. Get lost before I call the cops. *(Exits.)*

Ama: *(Laughs, howls like a wolf.)* She's mine, she likes me. *(Dances.)* She can't get enough of me. She'll meet me, I'll be waiting for her. *(Follows her off stage.)*

(The volcano flashes hotter, more thunder sounds, a mist rolls across the stage. Hula music starts then fades away. Enter Punia and Ama from opposite sides.)

Ama: Did you find one?

Punia: Of course. There was a lady selling them out of her van in the parking lot. What do you think? *(Holds out coral necklace.)*

Ama: It's perfect. Now I just have to find the vendor with those fancy drinks. Did you see where he's set up tonight?

Punia: You mean Kukali?

Ama: You're kidding, that's his name?

Punia: Isn't that great? He's named after a magician and he creates magical drinks.

Ama: I wonder if he knows any potions.

Punia: Like a love potion?

Ama: Sure, you know, something that fans the flames of passion. Hey, maybe passion fruit . . .

Punia: It's worth asking.

Ama: If we can find him. Let's go. *(Both exit.)*

(Volcano dies down, mist remains, lights are dimmed as a full moon rises. Soft sounds of waves on a beach. Enter Ricky with guitar cases and Larry carrying bongo drums.)

Ricky: *(Sets down cases and shakes hands.)* Give me a minute, Larry. My hands are killing me. I think I'm getting blisters from carrying this stuff back and forth every night.

Larry: *(Sets down drums carefully.)* You'd think we'd be used to this by now, but I'm beat too.

Ricky: What a night. First it looked like a storm, then the volcano erupted.

Larry: Then there was a wind that blew sparks from the barbeque pit into the crowd.

Ricky: Pele's skirt caught an ember. I even warned her about that earlier, but did she listen to me?

Larry: Does she ever?

Ricky: She was dancing like she was possessed.

Larry: She looked like she wanted to kill all the men on the beach. She kept kicking sand in their faces.

Ricky: Yeah, I don't know where she learned that step. It didn't look traditional.

Larry: She managed to make it look graceful enough to fool the tourists.

Ricky: I know, unbelievable, they loved it.

Larry: What got into her tonight?

Ricky: I think it was that surfer. He's been showing up all week, offering her little gifts, compliments. He's going full hog.

Larry: What's wrong with him?

Ricky: Nothing. She's so used to chasing guys off, she doesn't know any other way to react.

Larry: You should talk to her.

Ricky: It doesn't help. She gets defensive immediately.

Larry: Did she get her heart broken before?

Ricky: No one ever got close enough.

Larry: You think this guy has a chance?

Ricky: If persistence counts for anything he has a great chance. Did you see where she went after the show? I haven't seen her for a while.

Larry: I saw her way down the beach. She was sitting and watching the waves.

Ricky: Let's get this gear stowed, then I'll go find her.

Larry: Want me to show you where she went?

Ricky: That's all right. Actually, I'll meet you back at the bonfire. *(Picks up cases and exits.)*

Larry: That's a deal. *(Grabs drums and exits.)*

(Sounds of waves on a beach. Enter Pele, who sits down, looking toward stage right, hugging her knees to keep warm. Enter Ama with a coconut drink and water bottle.)

Ama: Here you are. I've been looking all over for you. I brought you a drink. It's not hot, but I thought you might be thirsty. *(Sits next to Pele.)*

Pele: *(Dreamy.)* All that water, and I'm thirsty.

Ama: Dancing will do that. Where did you learn that step, anyway? I've never seen it before.

Pele: Hmmm? What step?

Ama: I swear, you were sending off sparks at your heels. Sand was flying everywhere.

Pele: *(Smiles.)* Sparks?

Ama: I must have seen ten guys rubbing sand out of their eyes.

Pele: I hope no one was hurt.

Ama: They were riveted.

Pele: What's in that drink?

Ama: I thought you'd never ask. Unfortunately, I can't tell you. It's a deep dark secret.

Pele: What happened, did you buy that from Kukali?

Ama: Yes, how did you know?

Pele: He always says his recipes are a deep dark secret. He likes people to think he's some kind of magician.

Ama: Well, I think he is. I tried one of these earlier and it tasted magic.

Pele: Magic, huh? Maybe I'll try a sip. *(Accepts the drink and sips.)*

Ama: Well, what do you think?

Pele: I think it is a beautiful night, I am tired and thirsty, and some punk surfer boy has kindly provided me with a cup of nectar of the gods. *(More sips.)*

Ama: Does that earn the punk surfer boy the privilege of your company?

Pele: Some privilege. I have been nothing but nasty to you and you keep coming back for more. *(Takes a long drink.)*

Ama: I'm a glutton for punishment, ask anyone.

Pele: Hey, there's something in the bottom of this. *(Finishes drink, then scoops out necklace, holding it up to inspect it in the moonlight.)*

Ama: Now I wonder how that got in there.

Pele: Kukali is known for putting a little something extra in all his concoctions.

Ama: I helped him a little with this one.

Pele: I figured you might have.

Ama: Here, hand it over and I'll rinse it off. *(Takes necklace and pours water from bottle over it. Shakes it gently and hands it back.)* There, no more sticky fruit juice on it.

Pele: Thank you. It's beautiful. Look how the moonlight warms it up.

Ama: It would look even better next to your skin. Can I help you?

Pele: I can do it. *(Struggles with it under her hair. Ama lifts her hair gently until she fastens it.)* There, what do you think?

Ama: I think my fiery dancer looks like a princess, no . . . a goddess.

Pele: I think my punk surfer boy is the kindest, most patient human I've ever met.

Ama: Would you let this kind, patient surf punk call you some time?

Pele: I would be delighted.

Ama: Then I would be honored, but first, I think I should teach you how to be a surf punk.

Pele: Do you mean it? You'd teach me how to surf?

Ama: I have to, it's my legal obligation as the local champion.

Pele: Did you win?

Ama: Only first place.

Pele: Wow! *(Throws arms around his neck.)*

Ama: . . . and here's my prize. *(Slowly takes her arms from around neck. Keeps one hand and stands, pulling Pele up. Gazes affectionately at her for a moment.)* Ready for your first lesson?

Pele: Now? But it's so late?

Ama: Who can sleep? Come on! *(Tugs her toward stage right.)*

Pele: But its cold!

Ama: The water is warm. *(As both near exit, Ricky and Larry enter.)*

Ricky: There you are, I've been looking all over for you. Where are you two going?

Pele: *(Hesitates, laughs.)* I'm going for my first surfing lesson.

Ricky: This late?

Pele: Who can sleep? *(Exits with Ama.)*

Ricky: There goes one lucky guy . . . with my little sister. What should I do? Should I stop her? Can I trust that guy? You know what, Larry? She's a big girl now and she's made her choice . . . finally. I say, nice catch, Pele. My work here is done. *(Exits.)*

Larry: *(Looks up at mountain.)* I wonder how long the volcano will be dormant this time. *(Glances back over shoulder after Ama and Pele, then exits, shaking head.)*

References

McCaughrean, Geraldine. "The Pig that Goes Courting—a Hawaiian Myth." *The Silver Treasure: Myths and Legends of the World.* New York: Margaret K. Elderberry Books, 1996. 81–85.

Theroux, Paul. "The Hawaiians." *National Geographic.* December 2002: 2–41.

Additional Reading

Cole, Joanna, ed. "How Ma-ui Fished up the Great Island (Hawaii)." *Best-Loved Folk Tales of the World.* New York: Anchor Books, 1982. 599–601.

Martin, Rafe. *The Shark God.* New York: Arthur A. Levine Books, 2001.

Sherman, Josepha, ed. "Kukali—A Magician from Hawaii." *Merlin's Kin: Tales of the Heroic Magician.* Little Rock, AR: August House, Inc., 1998. 108–111.

Wardlaw, Lee. *Punia and the King of the Sharks.* New York: Dial Books for Young Readers, 1997.

11

Original Story Plays

Story Adaptation

Now that students have learned how to adapt stories from so many different sources, they are ready to write something completely original. The class will cluster ideas as a group. As students hear each other's ideas and build on them, note them on the board in front of the class and then take a vote. Begin with the following series of questions and cluster their responses on the board so everyone can see.

> 1. **Who is the main character? Ask for a description of a character that tells their occupation.**
> 2. **Where will the play take place? Be specific.**
> 3. **What time period is the play? Is it modern, historical, or futuristic?**
> 4. **What will be the conflict?**

After brainstorming, have the class study the lists and choose their favorite answers. Then have a blind vote, which avoids popularity contests. It's also a good lesson in how democracy works. Everyone gets their say, but maybe not their way.

Once the four main concepts have been decided, create a rough outline of the story for the class to develop. This outline will include the main characters and plot line. Stop the outline when the students begin to suggest endings to the story because their assignment is to write their own endings. Each student needs a copy of the outline. If it has been typed into a computer (perhaps by a student volunteer), it is simple to print up copies for the class. It is also possible to connect the computer screen to a projector for the entire class to see as it is recorded. The advantage to projecting the outline is that students can copy the outline down as it develops and make notes for their own ideas on the same page.

Give students the following parameters to help them focus their endings. Their stories will be written as plays and entered into a contest. They will have a chance to receive feedback during a critique session before their final plays must be turned in. You will grade them, and the class can then choose from among the top three to five plays. The papers will be graded based on very specific factors, which will be explained in a moment.

The winning play or plays will be performed. Decide who the audience will be, whether it is another class in the same grade, a younger or older class, or an audience filled with parents. Tell students that they will have no budget to build sets or make costumes, so they must plan something that can be staged with found, donated, or borrowed items and costumes. They can choose to write a readers theatre script, choral reading, or a play script. Tell them where it will be staged, whether in a classroom or on a stage, and go over whatever limitations the space will have.

It is also a good idea to give students a word or page limit. For instance, the play *The Last Toll* in Chapter 2 is roughly 2,300 words, while *Mudluscious* in Chapter 1 is 950. Tell them that magazine submissions always have word limits and that this will be good practice for them. Better yet, request writer guidelines for *Read Magazine,* or for *Plays* (see Other Sources at the end of this chapter). If students write short pieces, then a performance could include several versions, perhaps a comedy and a tragedy based on the same original premise.

At this point, hand out the two forms provided at the end of this chapter: the critique guidelines and evaluation rubric. Review them with the class. During a critique students must wear two hats. They must wear the hat of fellow writers who are providing constructive criticism, and they must also wear the hat of an audience that is hoping to be entertained, surprised, frightened, and so on. Since there are so many things to think about, it is a good idea to assign different questions to different students within the critique circle. Students can concentrate better and it will save time. As each student shares his or her particular concern, others can comment if they have different opinions. The author must remain silent until the end of the session, at which point he or she can answer any questions that remain or ask his or her own. Remember, focus must remain on how to strengthen and improve the story, not the author.

The evaluation rubric shows students what they need to include when they write their own plays. In evaluating the plays, teachers will look for the basics of grammar, style, length, and format. In addition, points are earned for originality and clarity. Finally, the issues discussed during the critique should be addressed.

Once the plays are polished, critiqued, and evaluated, the best submissions will be given a formal reading. At the end of the readings, students choose their winner. Depending on the resources within the school, teachers decide whether to enlist the help of art or music specialists at this point. Cooperation among teachers sets a good example for the teamwork required of students. Students observe how teachers contribute their own special talents. In the same way, only a few students can star in the show, but the efforts of stage, costume, and sound crews can make or break a production.

Now that they understand the assignment, students are ready to write a short paragraph that will summarize the end of the story. They name the characters and decide whether their story will have a happy, sad, or funny ending. It is time to turn them loose on their own stories and plays.

Playwriting

The following example will show how wild this exercise can become. A class of third graders created the bones for a story together using the clustering technique. Their story was then drafted by a very talented writer (not this author, but a close personal friend) into a 2,000-word short story that was delightfully funny. The decisions made by the class answered the four clustering questions as follows.

---

1. The main character is a guard dog.
2. The dog guards the zoo. He lives in a kennel with his family—wife and puppies. They belong to a long line of dogs that have guarded the zoo for years.
3. The story is set in modern times.
4. The conflict is that some kidnappers try to take a rare panda bear from the zoo, and they must be stopped.

The fun began as the characters took shape. First, the guard dog needed specifics. He became an Australian shepherd mix because one of the students insisted they were very good guard dogs because her family owned one. The dog in the story was named Agent Eleven because he was the Eleventh in a long line of offspring born to the original guard dog (Agent One). Agent Eleven became a family man with a litter of new puppies who loved to hear stories about their famous ancestors.

Armed with this information, the story was drafted. The author had to make many decisions, just as we will in order to adapt the story into a play. The next box presents a paragraph that summarizes the students' decisions and the outcome of the story.

> Three clumsy and stupid men disguised as groundskeepers plan to kidnap a rare panda. They circle the panda exhibit. The guard dog is on the lookout for lost children, but he gets suspicious when he notices the groundskeepers aren't emptying any of the trashcans. Agent Eleven overhears their plan and waits for the kidnappers to act. As the kidnappers slip into the enclosure, the dog follows them. All three men end up in the panda cage trying to lure it out, so the dog closes the gate behind them and traps them while he goes for help. He saves the day.

Since there were three kidnappers, the writer decided they would act like the Three Stooges. The story was suddenly a comedy. The kidnappers were clumsy and stupid and spoke very bad English. One was the leader and very bossy. They were given names right out of gangster movies: Bugsy, Mugsy, and Tugsy. Since Bugsy was the leader, they became the Bugsy Gang.

In the short story, Agent Eleven was asked by one of his restless puppies to tell a story, their favorite story about their father. The rest of the story becomes a flashback. This can be accomplished on stage with a simple scene change. The first scene has puppies playing in the zoo kennel while their parents watch. It is bedtime. The scene ends as Agent Eleven begins the story. If the family scene is performed in front of a curtain, then when this scene is over, the curtain can rise to reveal the panda cage at the zoo. If there is no curtain, the small family of puppies can play on the whole stage in the beginning, while the rest of the stage is empty. At the end of the introductory scene, the group remains on stage because Agent Eleven becomes the narrator for the rest of the play. As he begins his story, the simple stage is set up in the background. The puppies will settle into a small circle at one side of the stage to listen and watch.

To simplify staging decisions, assume the play will be staged in a grade school auditorium that doubles as a gym. There is a small raised stage, no lights, and a black curtain that creates a backstage area. Since the stage is raised, the puppies will arrange themselves in front of it at audience level just before the kidnappers appear. This will introduce the story within a story. Placing cast members at audience level also draws the audience into the story.

Costumes must be improvised. The dogs will wear face paint and plain brown clothing. Any female "dogs" that have long hair can wear it in high ponytails to look like floppy ears. The pandas will also wear face paint and black-and-white clothing, while the kidnappers will wear jeans and matching T-shirts with the word "groundskeeper" (preferably misspelled) written across the back with marker. When they return at night for the crime, they wear black T-shirts for camouflage.

Consider the stage set. How can a minimal stage turn into a zoo with a panda exhibit, a gate, and a U-Haul truck? The groundskeepers can borrow a rolling trash can from the school cafeteria. Posters will help set the scene. One will read "Zoo" and be taped to a side wall with an arrow pointing to the stage. Another poster will be taped to the back of a chair on stage and will read "Pandas." Streamers between this chair and another one nearby will create the barrier to the panda exhibit. This row of streamers creates a visual barrier while not actually blocking the view. Action will not take place behind it but will move around it.

One more poster with "U-Haul" printed in large orange letters will be carried on stage by a gangster, while the other two will walk behind him with the rolling trash can. The poster will be dropped flat on the stage once "the coast is clear," and they go for the pandas.

Further refinements can be made as the play unfolds. Since the short story is titled "Agent Eleven and the Bugsy Gang," we'll call the play adaptation *Agent Eleven: Guard Dog Extraordinaire.*

AGENT ELEVEN: GUARD DOG EXTRAORDINAIRE

Summary

What makes Agent Eleven extraordinary? He is a famous guard dog who foiled a gang of panda kidnappers at the zoo. His puppies love hearing the story, told with a sprinkling of fatherly bravado mixed with a generous portion of silliness.

Set

One poster reads "Zoo" and is taped to the side of the stage; another is taped to a chair and reads "Pandas." Two chairs create the front barrier of the panda exhibit, with two lines of paper streamers tied between them.

Props

A large, rolling trash can, three push brooms, one poster with "U-Haul" printed in large letters, a roll of duct tape, several branches of bamboo.

Costumes

"Dogs" wear face paint and brown clothing. Three "pandas" wear face paint and black-and-white clothing. Three kidnappers wear jeans and white T-shirts with "grondkeper" written across the back, then later pull on black T-shirts. Ned wears jeans and a brown shirt. The police officers wear navy blue.

Characters

Australian Shepherd Mix Dogs:

    Agent Eleven *(father)*
    Clarice *(a puppy)*
    Spike *(a puppy)*
    Several other puppies
    Mrs. Eleven *(mother)*
    Three panda bears

Humans:
    Bugsy
    Mugsy
    Tugsy
    Ned *(security guard)*
    Two police officers

AGENT ELEVEN: GUARD DOG EXTRAORDINAIRE

Scene 1

(Mrs. Eleven and Agent Eleven lie front stage left with eyes closed. Puppies chase each other, wrestle, roll, and do somersaults. Spike stops in front of Agent Eleven, studies him a minute, then sits and speaks.)

Spike: Daddy?

Agent Eleven: *(Opens eyes.)* Yes, dear one?

Spike: Can you tell us the story about the panda kidnappers?

Agent Eleven: *(Sits up.)* That's a wonderful idea.

Spike: Hey guys, *(Other puppies freeze.)* Daddy's going to tell the story about the panda kidnappers! *(Puppies rush to sit together in front of the stage, piling on top of each other, curling up in balls, wiggling.)*

Agent Eleven: *(Clears throat and paces.)* Are you sure you'd like to hear the panda story?

All puppies together: Oh yes, Daddy, please!

Agent Eleven: Very well. Let's start at the beginning. As you well know, you come from a long line of famous guard dogs. *(Puppies nod, some puff up their chests proudly.)*

Mrs. Eleven: *(Rolls over then sits up.)* Oh, puleeze, Eleven. Not that story again. If I hear that story one more time, I'll howl.

Puppies: Yes! Please! Oh, please, Daddy, please?

Mrs. Eleven: *(Stands and stretchs.)* Fine, fine. I think it's just about time for my shift to start anyway. Here comes Ned. I'll see you later, darlings.

Agent Eleven: Bye. Say good-bye to your mother, kids.

Puppies: Bye, bye, see ya later . . . bye . . .

Agent Eleven: Oh, Dear? Would you keep your nose to the ground for that bone? I know I saw it thrown into the bushes by the panda gate, but I haven't found it yet.

Mrs. Eleven: I'll sniff around for it. Bye. *(Exits.)*

Agent Eleven: Right. Well then, where was I? Oh, yes, the panda incident . . . long line of famous . . . *(Clears throat again.)* I am Agent Eleven. My father, your grandfather, was

Agent Ten. Our family of Australian shepherd mix lineage has guarded the other animals at the zoo for many years. When your grandfather retired, I took over the job.

Spike: And great, great, great, great grandfather helped capture the notorious bank robbers Bonny and Clyde Barrow, right Daddy?

Agent Eleven: That's right, he did, Spike. Now, who can tell me the most important thing for a guard dog?

All puppies together: You have to keep your eyes and ears open all the time!

Clarice: Because you never know when you'll hear something important!

Agent Eleven: Ah, good, you've been listening. Very good. Well, it all started one afternoon in July. *(Paces.)* I was making my rounds at the zoo. My job was to look for lost children and keep an eye out for troublemakers. Sometimes I'd let the children pet me if they were quiet and nice. Suddenly . . . *(Freezes and hugs corner of stage.)* . . . as I rounded the corner of the panda bear cage, I saw . . . *(Enter Bugsy, Mugsy, Tugsy.)* There was something funny about them. For one thing, they were terrible sweepers.

Mugsy: *(Pushes trash can while looking around.)* You see anything, boss?

Tugsy: *(Pushes broom in continuous circles around the others, bent over and studying ground intently.)* I never seen so much dirt before in my life. I wish I had one of these at home. What do you call this again, boss?

Bugsy: *(Carries broom like walking stick.)* It's a broom, Tugsy. What's the matter wit chu? *(Smacks Tugsy on the back of the head as he goes by.)* I never seen no one sweep like that. Ain't you never done it before?

Tugsy: *(Straightens and rubs head.)* Sure, boss, I just ain't never had no chance to look like a professional sweeper before. *(Turns and bumps Mugsy with broom, he falls over trash can.)*

Bugsy: Hey, Tugsy, watch what you're doin'. *(Tugsy swings back around and knocks Bugsy.)*

Tugsy: Oh, sorry, boss. *(Tosses broom behind back and reaches for Bugsy to help him up. Broom knocks Mugsy over again. Tugsy cannot lift Bugsy, falls on him.)*

Bugsy: Get offa me, you big meatloaf. *(Scrambles to feet, brushes off.)* I shoulda listened to my cousin, Frankie. He said you two were nuthin' but trouble, but I had to go and get all sentimental about family and you needin' jobs to feed your babies. . . . I bet you don't even have any babies, do you?

Mugsy: *(Picks up can.)* Sure boss, I got me some babes. There's Zelda, Lola, Mary Beth . . .

Tugsy: *(Brushes off.)* He said babies, not babes, you dope. Right, boss?

Mugsy: Babes, babies, what's the difference?

Bugsy: Mugsy, old man, you'd know the difference if you weren't the dumbest, clumsiest, noisiest, goofup I ever met. Now shaddup, both of you. I'm trying to think. Them pandas is somewheres and I aim to find 'em and get the lay of the land, see?

Mugsy: Sure boss, I'll look too.

Tugsy: Shhhh! He said quiet!

Mugsy: *(Shoves Tugsy.)* You be quiet.

Tugsy: *(Shoves back.)* No, you!

Bugsy: *(Threateningly.)* Gentlemen . . .

Mugsy: Right, boss.

Tugsy: Sorry, boss. *(All three circle around stage, slowly, forget trash can.)*

Agent Eleven: *(Walks downstage toward puppies.)* I decided to keep an eye on them.

Spike: Daddy, how come they didn't know you were watching them?

Agent Eleven: Well son, I was very careful. I followed and watched them from behind bushes and garbage cans. *(Creeps toward can and sniffs it.)* That's when I noticed that they weren't emptying the garbage cans either. Very suspicious, I watched as they circled the panda exhibit and became very interested in the door at the back that was for the zookeepers only. The three men sat down to take a break. *(Three sit in circle.)* I inched through the bushes until I was close enough to hear. *(Crawls back toward gang, crouches low.)*

Tugsy: *(Rubs feet.)* Hey, Bugsy? How long do we have to pretend to be sweepers here? My feet are killing me.

Bugsy: Shaddup, I'm telling ya! Why don't ya make an announcement on the loudspeakers? Attention Zoo guards! The Bugsy Gang is planning a heist! I don't care about your stinking feet. We gotta check out dis joint.

Mugsy: *(Pants, wheezes.)* Tugsy's right, Bugsy. I ain't used to this much exercise. When can we go home?

Bugsy: Listen, you bums. If I didn't need you to help me with those pandas . . . *(Looks around suspiciously.)* Like I said before, those pandas are worth a lot of dough, see? If we can get 'em out of here wit'out bein' caught, we'll be rich!

Agent Eleven: *(Quietly to puppies.)* So, I knew then that they planned to kidnap the pandas. But of course I had no proof and couldn't tell anyone yet. I would have to handle this myself. That was my job. I listened for more.

Bugsy: I checked out the lock. It looks easy enough. We'll have a talk with the zookeeper when he comes out. I'm sure he'll be happy to give us the key, right Mugsy?

Mugsy: Right, boss. Then I tranquilize the panda, and you drive up that U-Haul truck we ripped off, right boss? Nighty, night, panda! *(Snorts and slaps knee, falls over. Tugsy pushes the garbage can behind Bugsy, waiting to go.)*

Bugsy: Get up you clumsy doofus! How we gonna sneak in if you keep goofin' around? You think you can drive that heap without killin' us, Tugsy? *(Turns around to find Tugsy, falls into the garbage can. Head and legs stick out. Hollers until Tugsy and Mugsy pull out, then smacks them both on the head and stomps off. The other two trot to keep up. All exit.)*

Clarice: They're gonna steal the panda, Daddy. You have to stop them.

Spike: He knows that Clarice, don't worry. Just listen.

Agent Eleven: *(Smiles knowingly, walks back toward puppies and swings legs over stage to sit. Ned, Bugsy, Mugsy, and Tugsy mime the following as Agent Eleven narrates.)* Well, I knew their plan, but how could I stop them? I thought about the inside of the panda cage and had an idea. That night as they closed the zoo, I waited in the bushes near the zookeeper's door. *(Enter Ned.)* I watched zookeeper Ned unlock the door and go in to make sure there was plenty of bamboo for them to eat. While he was inside, the Bugsy Gang returned in a U-Haul truck. *(Enter Mugsy carrying a poster that says "U-Haul." Bugsy and Tugsy walk behind him, making car and truck noises with their mouths. Bugsy pushes the wheeled garbage can. All stop, Mugsy drops poster.)*

Bugsy: Right! Now where's the duct tape, Tugsy?

Tugsy: I thought Mugsy had it.

Mugsy: No way—it was Tugsy's job!

Bugsy: Shaddup you two! *(Reaches into can and pulls out tape.)* Here it is, you bums. *(Reaches back in and pulls out bamboo.)* And here's the bamboo. *(Hands a branch to each.)* Now let's just wait for our friend, Mr. Zookeeper, to come out.

Agent Eleven: *(Others continue to mime on stage.)* The three went over to the panda exhibit and lounged around. Minutes later, Ned came out. Bugsy walked up and asked for directions to the exit. Mugsy jumped out of the bushes and grabbed Ned from behind. The three men quickly taped up his mouth and stuck him in the wheeled garbage can. They pushed it into the bushes where no one would see it. *(They push it offstage.)* They looked around and then slipped into the enclosure. *(Creeps behind chairs and streamers as if it is a hallway.)* I rushed forward and stuck my paw out to catch the door. I heard whispers moving away from me and slipped in, listening.

Mugsy: Gee, boss, it's pretty dark in here.

Tugsy: Ooh, is widdo Mugsy afraid of da dark?

Bugsy: Shaddup! How many times do I gotta tell ya? Shaddup, I said.

Tugsy: Sorry boss.

Mugsy: *(Whines quietly.)* Sorry boss, but I still don't like the dark.

Bugsy: *(Enter three pandas, who sit, unaware of the gang, beyond the "hallway.")* We gotta get one of them bears back here. You, Mugsy! Get da bear. *(Shoves him toward pandas. Tugsy looks cautiously after him.)*

Mugsy: Here's one boss. Now what do I do?

Bugsy: Use the bamboo like I told ya, ya lug nut. It's like candy to 'em. One bite and the sleeping potion will knock him out. Hold it out and get one to follow you. Once you're out of the cage, let him have it. Make it quick like.

Mugsy: Okay, boss. Whatever you say, boss! *(In a singsong voice.)* Here little panda bear . . . I have nice, sweet bamboo for you . . .

(Three pandas watch Mugsy come toward them waving bamboo. The pandas approach Mugsy and back him up against the back wall, sitting and watching him. Mugsy cowers, but holds out branch. They take leaves and munch them, watching him.)

Agent Eleven: Tugsy was gone for several minutes. Bugsy became impatient.

Bugsy: Mugsy—go find out what's taking him so long.

Agent Eleven: Mugsy hesitated and then slowly went into the cage. Then I heard . . .

Mugsy: Boss! They got Tugsy cornered! They don't look too sleepy to me. You sure that was sleeping juice, boss? *(Pandas turn as he enters and all stand.)* Whoa! Nice little teddy bears . . . *(One comes toward him.)* Yikes! *(Backs away.)* I don't like the way they're looking at me. . . . Boss? You hear me, boss? *(Panda follows.)* Nice little bear . . . *(Runs, moaning; panda chases like it's a game.)*

Bugsy: Nuts! What's all that racket? I'm coming in there. Why do I gotta do everything around here? You better not be running away from those pandas. That was not the plan . . .

Agent Eleven: I'd been waiting for this. I leaped up and hit the handle. The gate slammed shut. They were trapped! Then I ran outside and found Ned. I pushed over the can and he rolled out. *(Ned rolls out onto stage.)* He was on the walkie-talkie before he even stood up.

Ned: *(Talks into headset.)* Yeah, this is Ned over at the Panda Pound. Get me some back up, pronto! Agent Eleven just trapped some thugs in the building. . . . Never mind what I was doing. . . . That's right. . . . No, I'm fine.

Agent Eleven: Ned straightened up slowly, rubbing his back. *(Walks over to Ned and sits by him.)*

Ned: Hey, boy, where'd you come from?

Agent Eleven: Woof!

Ned: You got that Bugsy Gang trapped inside all by yourself?

Agent Eleven: Woof!

Ned: Well, let's go take a look. Come on, boy. *(Both turn toward pandas and gang. Ned laughs, Agent Eleven barks. Tugsy is against the back wall, waving bamboo at pandas to fend them off, Bugsy runs still, and Mugsy is flat on the floor kicking and crying while a panda sits on his back.)*

Ned: Hey, boy, I think Wanda likes that one, don't you?

Agent Eleven: Woof, woof! Awwwooo! *(Turns to puppies.)* I guess Wanda was lonely.

(Enter two police officers.)

Joe: Now how did they get in there?

Ned: I'm not exactly sure. They stuffed . . . well, never mind. Let's just say I didn't see it, but ol' Eleven here sure didn't miss a thing. Looks like he simply locked them in once they were all occupied.

Jim: That one doesn't look too happy. Why is he running around?

Ned: Beats me.

Bugsy: Hey, you! In the brown shirt! *(Ned points to himself, questioningly.)* Yeah, you. What are you waiting for? Let me out before this overgrown fuzz ball takes a bite out of me!

John: *(To Ned.)* How'd he know Fuzzy's name?

Ned: That's not Fuzzy, that's Paulette and she's lonely just like Wanda.

Jim: What do lonely pandas do?

Ned: Mostly they just like to use their boyfriends for seat cushions.

Bugsy: Hey! Back off, Fuzzy! *(Paulette catches him in a bear hug, wrestles him to the ground, and sits on him. Ned, Joe, Jim all laugh, Agent Eleven barks.)*

Joe: *(Wiping tears from his eyes.)* Well, come on guys, looks like those thugs have had enough. The party's over. Maybe we better get Wanda off that guy. He doesn't look too good.

(Police coax pandas away from gang and lead gang offstage.)

Agent Eleven: The police led the crooks away in handcuffs, with Bugsy complaining loudly.

Bugsy: I knew this was a dumb idea. We shoulda stuck wid stealin' cars!

Agent Eleven: Jim gave me a good scratch behind the ears and said . . .

Jim: Eleven, you've done a fine job once again. I'm going to put you in for a medal.

Clarice: And to this very day, Daddy, there's a big statue of you by the front gate that says . . .

Spike and Clarice together: Agent Eleven, whose courage, bravery, and cleverness saved our panda bears from the notorious Bugsy Gang.

Agent Eleven: That's right, little ones. Now everyone, time for bed.

(Puppies, stretch, yawn, and settle down to sleep. Enter Mrs. Eleven.)

Mrs. Eleven: My goodness—how did you ever get them all asleep so early?

Agent Eleven: Oh, just a little story.

Mrs. Eleven: About their father, the hero?

Agent Eleven: Of course, my dear. By the way, did I ever tell you about the time I single-handedly captured Al Capone when he tried to kidnap some baby penguins? But that's another story . . . *(Two exit together.)*

Other Sources

Writers guidelines for play scripts can be obtained from the following sources:

Read Magazine:
200 First Stamford Place
P.O. Box 120023
Stamford, CT 06912-0023

Plays:
http://www.playsmag.com/ply/static/submissionsguidelines.html

Form 11.1

Critique Guidelines

1. What concerns does the author of the play have? Who is the author's target audience?

2. What is the best thing about the play? Be specific. Was there a character, description, section of dialog, scene, or something else that you thought was interesting? Why?

3. What is your overall reaction to the story? Was it fun? Was it scary, silly, romantic, exciting, or slow?

4. Does the opening scene grab your attention? Does it make you care about what will happen?

Form 11.1 *Continued*

5. Are there any questions you would like answered within the story? Do you want to know what happened after a certain event or why characters reacted the way they did? Are there characters you would like to know more about or ones that seem unnecessary?

6. Listen to the flow of action. Is it logical for characters to be in certain places? Are there clear transitions explaining how characters get from one place to another?

7. Is the time frame consistent? Do the characters remain in their period setting or do modern expressions or characteristics sneak in? Is the time of day and day of the week always understood? If there are flashbacks or imaginary sequences, are they clearly set apart?

8. Do the voices of the characters reflect their personalities? Do characters act their ages? Does the conflict change the main characters' behavior, personality, etc.? (It should.) Does the change remain consistent? How are other characters affected and is the change appropriate?

Form 11.1 *Continued*

9. Who is telling the story? If the narrator changes, is there a good reason? Are the transitions clear?

10. Does the dialog sound natural? Do accents change?

11. Does the dialog reveal the personalities of the characters? What main characteristic describes each character, or are some fuzzy? Are characters too simple—good or evil, happy or sad, brave or scared—rather than a little of everything like real people?

12. Is the ending satisfactory? Did it answer questions, raise interesting new ones, solve the conflict or leave you wondering?

Congratulate the author on a great effort.

Original Story Plays

Form 11.2
Play Evaluation Rubric

Title _____

Author _____

Grade _____

	Beginning 1	Developing 2	Accomplished 3	Exemplary 4	Score
Story	The plot is clear.	The story is original.	The point of view is consistent.	The beginning is captivating.	
Flow	The historical period is consistent.	The time frame makes sense.	Transitions are smooth.	The ending is satisfactory.	
Characters	Personalities are clear.	Characters are likeable.	Dialog is natural.	Characters change.	
Language	Nouns and their adjectives are clear.	Verbs agree with their nouns.	Verb tense does not change.	Verbs are active.	
Grammar	Spelling is correct.	Punctuation is correct.	Word limit is met.	Text is double-spaced and indented.	
Staging	The set is appropriate to the space.	Costumes are simple yet appropriate.	Props can be made or acquired within budget.	Stage directions are clear.	
Critique	Author is cooperative and helpful.	Questions are answered.	Corrections are made.	Problems are solved.	

May be copied for classroom use. *Literary Ideas and Scripts for Young Playwrights* by Lisa Kaniut Cobb (Portsmouth, NH: Teacher Ideas Press) © 2004.

Glossary

Adaptation—A story that is based on source material such as poetry, jokes, or myths. Parts of the source material are changed or embellished with new details to create a new version.
Antagonist—The person in a story who is an opponent of the protagonist; also known as the bad guy.
Anthropomorphic—A character in a story that is an animal who acts like a human.
Anticlimactic—Something that happens after the main conflict in a story is resolved. It is not as important to the story as the climax.
Assonance—The repetition of sounds in a series of words.
Backdrop—A large cloth with a scene painted on it that hangs at the back of a stage.
Clustering—A technique for gathering ideas and making decisions while planning a story.
Dialog—The words spoken by characters in a play.
Expand—To expand a story or poem means to create details and background information that were not included in the original.
Irony—A situation created in a drama that is unexpected.
Lyrics—The words that are sung in a song.
Metaphor—Words, characters, or a situation that have more than their literal meaning in a story. Metaphors can broaden the implications of words and actions by placing them in a wider context.
Modernize—To rewrite a story that is set in the past by setting it instead in the present.
Motivation—The emotion or desire that drives a character to act in a play or story.
Pacing—The quickness or slowness of actions, words, or syllables that move a story from beginning to end.
Perspective—The way a situation appears to the character in a story or play.
Point of View—Similar to perspective, except that in a play, each character gets to present his or her own views through the dialog.
Protagonist—The main character in a play or story; also known as the good guy.
Public Domain—Work that has been published for which the copyright has expired. Such work is available for adaptation by others.
Redeeming Qualities—The qualities in a character's personality that make him or her likeable.
Rivalry—A competition between characters who are each striving for the same thing or who oppose each other.
Scenario—A situation that affects the characters in a play or story and that leads to a sequence of events.
Script—The written text of a play that includes dialog, stage directions, and notes for the production of the play.

Stereotypes—Oversimplified characters that are one dimensional and conform to a general expectation, such as the dumb blond or the brilliant scientist.

Story Elements—Parts of a story such as the historic setting, financial circumstances, character types, and plot events that affect and change the characters and their actions.

Symbolism—The use of words or objects to suggest meanings that aren't expressed literally.

Tension—The conflict that motivates characters to act, or a situation that motivates characters. Usually it forces the characters to make decisions they might otherwise try to avoid.

Well-rounded Characters—Characters that have good or redeeming qualities as well as bad or weak qualities, making them more realistic and complex. They are the opposite of stereotypes.

Index

Analyzing a theme, 29
Antagonists, changing, 74
Anthropomorphic animals, 73
Anticlimactic endings, 89

Backdrop paintings, 88, 111, 120
Budget, working with none, 29

Carroll, Lewis, "The Walrus and the Carpenter," 9
Chorus parts, 3
Clustering: the concept, xi; form, 81; an original story, 157; setting limits, 19; steering decisions, 100
Comic relief, 60
Conflict: clustering, xi; finding a story's, 19
Constructive criticism, 51
Contests, purpose of, x
Copyright, 1
Cummings, E. E., "in Just-," 2

Energizing writing assignments, ix
Exploring cultural differences, 73
Extension activities, 17, 71, 97

Feelings, respecting others', ix
Frost, Robert, "The Road Not Taken," 99

Ground rules for student playwrights, 29

"Hansel and Gretel" adaptation, 38; modernized, 77
Hawaiian myth adaptation, 138
Historical sources, 119

"In Just-," 2
Interpersonal skills and writing teams, 51

"Jack and the Beanstalk" adaptation, 29
Joke sources, 97

Leading questions, 74
Learning styles, x

Motivation, finding character, 19
Mythology, as a source for cultural ideals, 137

Pace, maintaining in a play, 1, 111
"Paul Revere" adaptation, 122
Permissions, 1
Playwriting, developing language arts skills, x
Plot adjustments, 88
Poe, Edgar Allan, "The Raven," 108
Poems: adapting, 1; enhancing the experience, 99
Predictable characters, 76
Prewriting, 29; planning sheet for, 48
Public domain, 1

"The Raven," 108
Readers theatre: explanation of, x; other sources, 28; scripts, 21, 53
Redeeming qualities in characters, 76
Rehearsals and critiques, 51
"The Road Not Taken," 99

Setting: "Snow White" in New York, 59; to suit new characters, 51
"Snow White" adaptation, 59
Sound effects, 89, 111, 121
Source of writing material, ix, x; fairy tales, 19, 29, 51, 59, 73; story jokes as, 87
Stage hands, 12
Stereotypes, 73
Story adaptation, x
Summary paragraph, 74
Surprise endings, 52
Suspense, 52

Teamwork among students and teachers, 158
Tension building, 3
Theme analysis, 29
"The Three Billy Goats Gruff" adaptations, 21, 53

Universal themes, 73

Viewpoint: different, 19; shifted, 20

"The Walrus and the Carpenter," 9
"What if" games, 19

About the Author and the Illustrator

About the Author

Lisa Kaniut Cobb grew up in Michigan, met her husband in Boston, and married him in New Haven, Connecticut. They settled in Cleveland, Ohio, started a family, and sixteen years later they all moved to Denver, Colorado, where they feel like natives—they've been there a whole five years. Lisa worked as a freelance technical editor and writer for twenty years, while raising her three children. She also spent many hours as a volunteer, teaching art education and writing at the lower- and middle-school levels—all of which led Lisa back to graduate school at the University of Denver. Her master's degree is in creative writing. Her experiences in the classroom and her love of the theater led to the writing program presented in this book. Her students enthusiastically tackled the exercises, confirming Lisa's belief that this approach to teaching writing is worth pursuing. Lisa hopes the lessons in her first book will help teachers bring the excitement of the stage into their classrooms and into their student's hearts.

About the Illustrator

Helen Matthews has always loved art. Her interest in illustration came from writing and drawing stories for her children when they were small. After they were grown, she took art classes at the Curtis Art Center in Greenwood Village, Colorado. These are her first published illustrations. Helen would like to thank her drawing teacher, Rick Brogan, for all his help. Helen lives with her husband, Dennis, and dog, Mischief, in Denver, Colorado.